CONVERSATIONS WITH...
MEISTER ECKHART

With love,

Sheda xx

July 2010

CONVERSATIONS WITH...
MEISTER ECKHART

SIMON PARKE

Conversations with... Meister Eckhart

White Crow Books is an imprint of
White Crow Productions Ltd
PO Box 1013
Guildford GU1 9EJ

www.whitecrowbooks.com

Text design and eBook production by Essential Works
www.essentialworks.co.uk

ISBN 978-1-907355-18-9
eBook ISBN 978-1-907355-61-5
Audiobook ISBN 978-1-907355-42-4

Religion & Spirituality

Distributed in the UK by
Lightning Source Ltd.
Chapter House
Pitfield
Kiln Farm
Milton Keynes MK11 3LW

Distributed in the USA by
Lightning Source Inc.
246 Heil Quaker Boulevard
LaVergne
Tennessee 37086

Contents

Preface

The conversation presented here is imagined; but Eckhart's words are not. All of Eckhart's words included here are his own, taken from his writings and teachings. The questions recorded are sometimes mine; used for dramatic effect or to clarify what is being said. But equally often they are Eckhart's own, as he would often ask himself questions and then answer them! If sometimes there is an air of comedy, then it is in keeping with Eckhart's own undoubted comic touch and startling use of language and ideas. No wonder he caused offence.

The only alteration to his original words has been the occasional addition of a link word to help the flow; or once or twice, the removal of a sub-clause in a sentence, to aid clarity. But such amendments never alter Eckhart's meaning. After all, to discover his meaning is the reason for this adventure; and so these are his words. Yes, even the bit about the angel called Conrad...

Introduction

The hooded figure before me is about to make the last journey of his life. The year is 1327, and at the age of 68, Meister Eckhart is about to walk the 500 miles from Strasburg to Avignon, to defend himself before the Pope against charges of heresy. Powerful people, including the Archbishop of Cologne, have been upset by his fresh and original talk of God and the soul, and want him denounced. They wish for him to be declared a heretic, a despiser of truth; perhaps even burned at the stake. Eckhart himself is well aware that only seventeen years ago, Margaret Porete had been imprisoned and the burned at the stake in Paris for her mystical writings concerning the fusion of God and the human soul. And Eckhart was saying much that was the same. He has a powerful body, and robust for a man his age. It has certainly been a working body. As a Dominican leader, he has travelled miles on foot across Europe, attending meetings as far apart as Strasburg, Toulouse and Piacenza. Now, however, he is still, and his head bowed. He wears a white tunic and scapular cap, with black cloak and hood. It is the familiar dress of the Dominican order, of which Eckhart has been a member since the age of 15. It is this order, founded in 1215 by St Dominic, which has educated him and given him the platform for his public ministry – a ministry in which he has shone as academic, philosopher, pastor, preacher and mystic.

I look around from my position in these Rhineland cloisters. On the eastern side of the cloister, novice monks are being taught. On the south side, there is book work taking place; monks skilled in calligraphy creating new theological tomes for the monastery library. I arrived late yesterday evening, and have been well looked after. I enjoyed some fish and beer in the kitchen, before retiring to bed. The monks all sleep clothed, in dormitories; but I am staying in the guest house for travellers and pilgrims, where we are allowed to undress.

Of course, the monastery day is shaped around the eight

offices or services: Matins at 2.00am; Lauds at 5.00am; Prime at 7.00am; Terce at 9.00am; Sext at midday; None at 3.00pm; Vespers at 5.00pm and Compline at 8.00pm. These services include prayers, chanting of psalms, bible reading and singing. In the course of the week, all 150 psalms will be sung. No wonder these services are called 'The Work of God'; they are a labour. Yet the monks seem happy enough. As one said to me this morning: 'Self-will has no scope here. Food is scanty, and our garments rough. Oh yes – and then when sleep is sweetest, we must rise at the bell's bidding! But this is also true – everywhere there is peace, serenity and a marvellous freedom from the tumult of the world.'

Much of Eckhart's life has been spent in a monastery, though not all. The 'Meister' in his name means 'Master', and is an academic title from the University of Paris, where he was twice regent master. He is also an admired and trusted member of the Dominican Order, who on several occasions has been sent to reform ailing priories. Such postings have taken him to Saxony, Strasburg and now most recently, to Cologne. A further string to his bow has been as spiritual counsellor. Over the years, he has proved a safe haven for many who have sought God in their life, but found themselves troubled by the state of the institutional church. In a century of flowering female spirituality, he has been a supportive figure for many Dominican nuns and women in the burgeoning lay communities that have arisen.

So a full life indeed; and one of which any man might be proud. Yet in these twilight years, when he should be resting on his laurels, he is a man whose career and reputation are under threat; and from the very church he has served. How can this be? What has he said to anger the spiritual powers, that he must now plead his case before the Pope himself? This is what I hope to discover as we talk.

Certain things I am aware of, however, even now. The old man before me is no shrinking violet; and best known not for being a professor, but for being a preacher – an original preacher who uses his native German language to startling effect.

Eckhart preaches a spiritual vision which distrusts the artifice of both ritual and church dogma. Instead, he aims at nothing less the spiritual and psychological transformation of those given to his care. To this end, Eckhart makes the disposition of the human heart the key to all things; speaks very little of church ceremonies, and believes that outward penances have only limited value. He doesn't say 'Flee from the world!' as many churchmen have down the years. But intriguingly he does say 'Flee from your self!'

Controversially, he also says that God cannot be described; and that any attempt to do so is bound not only to fail, but also to harm. Indeed, he goes as far as to say in one sermon that 'We must take leave of God.'

No wonder he has faced the Church inquisition. But as a glance round Europe at this time reveals, the orthodox cause scarcely burns bright. The clergy and monasteries are in disarray; the Pope has fled from Rome to Avignon in his power battle with the Holy Roman Emperor Louis 4th; and the Inquisition are a hunting and torturing terror against all perceived error. It is not surprising, therefore, that across the continent, there has been a sharp rise in the number of lay groups, particularly female, seeking fresh ways of believing. And no wonder also that many of these have found a champion in Eckhart and teachers like him.

But perhaps more than discovering the origins of offence caused by Eckhart, I've come here to learn from the man myself. If he has helped others, then perhaps he can help me. Having read transcripts of his sermons, faithfully recorded by his followers, I'm aware that he can be challenging; but perhaps this will be good for me. He can certainly be hard to understand on occasion. Indeed, when first introduced to him, the advice I was given was this: 'Don't try and understand Eckhart. Don't try and work it all out; his is a vision not a system. Just read him. Just listen to him. And the truth will quietly do its own work.'

So this is what I hope, as I embark on my conversation. Eckhart has said many memorable things, of course. But now, as he sits gazing through the arches out on to the vegetable gardens beyond, I am reminded of his words about the eye: 'The eye with which I see God,' he once said, 'is the same eye with which God sees me.' It is intriguing statements like this – suggesting such union between the divine and the human – which make me glad I am able now to spend time with him, and learn. Yes, he must soon leave for Avignon, in order to defend himself before the Pope. But before that journey, I determine to make the most of my conversation... with Meister Eckhart.

ONE

Detachment

Since arriving at the monastery, I have been looked after by two kind women, Hildegaard and Magdalene. I was surprised to see them, and when I asked what brought them here, discovered they were members of the Beguines, who lived in the adjoining convent.

The Beguines were lay female communities across Europe, self-sufficient in themselves, and devoted to a common life of prayer and service. Many of these women have recently linked themselves to Dominican convents, attracted both by the quality of study here and the mystical character of the spirituality.

The Beguines include among their numbers many who are mystics and visionaries, and are known both for their love poetry to God and meditations on Christ. They write always in the vernacular, which causes trouble. The authorities prefer the faith taught in Latin, rather than in people's own language; and have become increasingly suspicious of the Beguines, believing their ways to be subverting the true faith.

Henry of Virneburg, the Archbishop of Cologne, is not alone in associating their mystical speculation with heresy; and in associating Eckhart with the Beguines. And so it was that last year, acting on the Archbishop's orders, the inquisition summoned Eckhart to explain his beliefs. This he had done, defending himself against charges of heresy. It was only last week, however, when the verdict went against him, that he used his magisterial status and made good his right to appeal to the Pope.

I am aware, therefore, that I speak with a man who has been condemned by his own. We have both attended Prime, and enjoyed a breakfast of bread and fruit. We now sit together in the

north cloister, which we've decided to make our home for the day.
The air is fresh, but with the clouds high, a warm day is promised.

s.p: Meister Eckhart, you are a renowned scholar, but perhaps
remain most famous for your teaching and preaching. And
when speaking to the religious communities in your care, like
the Beguines, you choose your native German over the more
traditional Latin.

Meister Eckhart seems surprised I should note this, but I continue.

I was honoured, of course, to hear you last night at *Vespers,*
and your listeners clearly appreciate your style and enjoy
listening to you very much.

m.e: If no one had been there, I should have had to preach
the sermon to the collection box!'

s.p: Well, I know you are a passionate teacher; though I didn't
realize you went so far as preaching to the church furniture.
But on behalf of all those who will never hear you, tell me:
when you stand up to preach, what do you say?

m.e: When I preach, I am accustomed to talk about
detachment, saying we should become free of ourselves and of
all things. Secondly, I say that we should be formed inwardly
back into simple goodness, which is God. Thirdly, I say that
we should be aware of the great nobility which God has given
to the soul in order that we should become wonderfully united
with him. Fourthly, I tell of the purity of the divine nature,
and of the radiance within it which is inexpressible.

s.p: Then those shall be our headings today! We shall consider
first detachment; then the spiritual life; then the soul and
finally, God – though I suspect he may be spoken of before
then! God doesn't fit that easily into our boxes – but aware

of your present trials, I would like to add one more heading to our dialogue, if I may – and that is suffering. Why do we suffer and how can we deal with suffering when it comes? I know this is an issue you have reflected on a great deal.

Eckhart nods and seems happy enough with this arrangement.

But first, tell me honestly, Meister Eckhart: don't you ever feel like giving up? I mean, *really!* Why live when your supposed friends treat you so poorly?

M.E: Why live? If there were an answer, it could be no more than this: 'I live only to live!' And that is because life is its own reason for being, springs from its own source, and goes on and on, without ever asking why; just because it is life. Thus, if you ask a genuine person – that is, one who acts uncalculatingly from his heart – 'Why are doing that?' he will reply in the only possible way: 'I do it because I do it!'

S.P: So you haven't given up on planet earth?

M.E: The earth perceives within itself that it is remote and different from heaven, which is why it has fled from heaven to the lowest point and is immoveable, so that it cannot approach heaven. But heaven has perceived within itself that earth has fled from it, and has taken up the lowest position. Therefore it pours the whole of itself into the earth to make it fertile, to the extent that the wide span of heaven retains not so much as a pin prick of its breadth but rather gives the whole of itself to the earth and makes it fertile. Therefore the earth is the most fertile of all temporal things.

S.P: I like that. I like the idea of heaven pouring the whole of itself into the cowering earth; that's a hopeful image. So perhaps we're ready now to consider detachment –

M.E: — It is the highest virtue —

S.P: So you say. So if detachment —

M.E: — or disinterest —

Eckhart was not shy of interrupting, if he wanted to clarify something.

S.P: — if these things, detachment or disinterest, are the highest virtue, that must mean you put them above love?

M.E: He who would be serene and pure needs but one thing: detachment.

S.P: That's a striking claim. What do you mean by it?

M.E: Human perfection consists in becoming distant from creatures and free from them; to respond in the same way to all things, not to be broken by adversity nor carried away by prosperity, not to rejoice more in one thing than another, not to be frightened or grieved by one thing more than another. You could not do better than to go where it is dark; that is, unconsciousness.

S.P: This is a radical detachment. Shouldn't we at least attach ourselves to some kind of holy knowledge?

M.E: A master says, (*Readers note: Eckhart often quotes from past teachers, referring to them as 'masters'*) To achieve the interior act one must assemble all one's powers as it were into one corner of one's soul, where, secreted from images and forms one is able to work. We must sink into oblivion and ignorance. In this silence, this quiet, the Word is heard. There is no better method of approaching this Word than in silence, in quiet: we hear it and know it aright in unknowing.

To one who knows nothing it is clearly revealed. Now you will object!

s.p: I must object, yes! For aren't you saying that human salvation lies in ignorance? Yet ignorance makes fools or brutes of us, surely?

m.e: This is transformed knowledge; not ignorance which comes from *lack* of knowing; it is by knowing that we get to this unknowing.

s.p: So we use our knowing to take us to unknowing?

m.e: The pupils of St Dionysius asked him why Timothy outstripped them in perfection? Dionysius said, 'Timothy is a God-receptive man. He who is expert at this outstrippeth all men.' In this sense, your unknowing is not a defect but your greatest perfection, and suffering your highest activity. Kill your activities and still your faculties if you would realize the birth of God in you.

s.p: Interesting. So is this the unknowing of innocence, perhaps? A return to some former time that we have now lost; a time before we existed even?

m.e: Let us be eternally as poor as we were when we eternally were not. Abiding in him in our essence we shall be what we are. We shall know God without any sort of likeness; love without matter, and enjoy without possession. We shall conceive all things in perfection.

The poor in spirit take leave of themselves and of all creatures: they are nothing, they have nothing, they do nothing; and these poor are not – save that by grace they are God with God: which they are not aware of.

*I am aware how dangerous these words are. Margaret Porete
had said something almost exactly the same; that the soul 'knows
only one thing: that she knows nothing, and wills only one thing:
that she does not will anything.' I keep this to myself however, as
Eckhart continues:*

I said once that whoever possesses the world least, actually
possesses it the most. No one owns the world as much as they
who have given the whole world up.

s.p: So let me understand: human perfection consists in
becoming more distant from things, so that we are able to
respond more freely to life?

s.p: People say: 'I so wish I stood as well with God as other
people; and had as much devotion and peace with God, as
other people seem to possess; and that I could be just like them
and as poor as them.' Or they say, 'The spiritual life doesn't
work for me unless I am in this or that particular place or do
this or that particular thing. I must go to somewhere remote or
live in a hermitage or a monastery!'

s.p: That's true. I do turn to holy places or holy activities
when circumstances are not favourable, hoping they'll get me
out of the mess.

m.e: Truly, it is you who are the cause of this mess yourself,
and nothing else.

s.p: So it's not my location which is the problem? I do often
think I'd be holier somewhere else; somewhere more suitable
for me and my gifts!

m.e: It is your own self-will; even if this doesn't seem to you
to be the case. The lack of peace that you feel can only come
from your own self-will, whether you are aware of this or not.

Whatever we think – that we should avoid certain things and seek out others, whether these be places or people, particular forms of devotion, this group of people or this kind of activity – these are not to blame. Rather, it is you as you exist in these things who holds yourself back; for you do not stand in proper relationship to them.

s.p: So how can I stand in proper relationship to my circumstances? That would be good to know.

m.e: Start with yourself, and take leave of yourself. Truly, if you do not depart from yourself, then wherever you take refuge, you will find difficulties and unrest, wherever it may be.

s.p: I've always wanted to live by the sea. And then of course a friend of mine believes she'll be happy if she's married.

m.e: Those who seek peace in external things, whether in places or devotional practices; people or works; in withdrawal from the world or poverty or self-abasement: however great these things may be or whatever their character, they are still nothing at all and cannot be the source of peace. Those who seek in this way, seek wrongly; and the further they range, the less they find what they are looking for. They proceed like a traveller who has lost their way: the further they go, the more lost they become.

s.p: It is hard when you feel thwarted by life.

m.e: When you are thwarted, it is your attitude that is out of order.

s.p: So what should such a person do? I feel thwarted in some measure every day!

M.E: First of all, they should renounce themselves, and then they will have renounced all things. Truly, if someone were to renounce a kingdom or the whole world, while still holding onto themselves – then they would have renounced nothing at all! Nothing! And inversely, if someone renounces themselves, then whatever they might keep – whether it be a kingdom or honour or whatever it may be – they will still have renounced all things.

S.P: It's about the quality of the heart; about the heart's intent.

M.E: St Peter said, 'See Lord, we have left everything!' when in fact he had left nothing more than a mere net and his little boat.

S.P: It was his living I suppose –

M.E: Whoever renounces their own will and their own self, renounces all things – as surely as if all things were in that person's possession to do with as they pleased; for what you do not wish to desire, you have handed over to God.

S.P: It's not about the life we handle; but how we handle the life.

M.E: 'Blessed are the poor in spirit' – which is to say those who are poor in will. Let no one be in any doubt about this: if there were a better way, then our Lord would have told us. 'If anyone would follow me, he must first deny himself.' This is the nub of the matter. Examine yourself, and wherever you find yourself, then take leave of yourself. This is the best way of all.

S.P: Some would say they already have renounced themselves; that they are now experienced spiritual travellers.

M.E: You should know that no one has ever renounced themselves so much in this life that there was nothing left of them to renounce. But in truth, there are few people who are properly aware of this, and who remain constant in their efforts. But it is a fair trade and equal exchange: to the extent that you depart from things, – no more and no less – God enters into you with all that is his; as far as you have stripped yourself of yourself in all things. It is here that you should begin, my friend, whatever the cost; for it is here you will find true peace, and nowhere else.

S.P: You're saying that peace is the fruit of inner renunciation; and that people can sometimes hide behind what they do outwardly, which is true. If someone says they're a nurse there is the assumption they are kind; but of course this isn't necessarily so. I've met some very unkind ones!

M.E: People should not worry about what they do, but about what they are. If they and their ways are good, then their deeds are radiant. However wonderful our works may be, they do not in any way make us holy in so far as they are works. Rather, it is we ourselves, in so far as we possess fullness of being, who sanctify our works, whether these be sleeping, eating, waking or anything at all.

S.P: It is the person who we are that makes good our acts?

M.E: Little comes from the works of those whose being is slight. This teaches us that we should make every effort to be good, and should worry not so much about what we do or the character of our actions. Rather, but we should be concerned about their ground.

S.P: So I need to ask myself about my motivations, which is hard because often I don't wish to consider those. What are the origins of this act in me? Is this my essence at work; or perhaps some part of me which is less pure?

M.E: The reason why a person's essence and ground – which lends goodness to their works – is wholly good, is that their mind is wholly turned to God. Make every effort then to let God be great and to ensure all your good intentions and endeavours are directed to him both in all that you do, and in all that you refrain from doing. If you seek God, then you will find both God and all goodness. Indeed, if you trod on a stone while in this state of mind, it would be a more godly act than if you were to receive the body of our Lord while being concerned only for yourself and having a less detached attitude of mind!

S.P: That's quite a thought. That all we have to do is look after our inner attitude; and that life is immediately good around us, and through us, whatever we are doing! It's the opposite of a vicious circle; it's a beautiful circle: virtue takes us to God; and God takes us to virtue.

M.E: Whoever holds to God, holds both to God and all virtue. And what was previously the object of your seeking, now seeks you; what you hunted, now hunts you; what you fled, now flees you. This is so because the things of God cling to those people who cling to God, and all those things flee them which are unlike God and alien to him.

S.P: If you don't mind me saying, it seems there are different sorts of mystics. Some preach a mysticism of love, in which the soul is caught up in a wonderful romance with God. You, however, preach a mysticism not of romance, but of emptiness. Could you perhaps reflect more on this? You talk about our need for nothingness, for instance. That can sound strange to people; offensive, even.

M.E: The deeper the well, the higher it is; for the height and depth are one. Thus whoever can humble themselves the more, the greater is their exaltation. For our entire being is founded purely on a process of becoming nothingness. Whoever desires to be given everything must first give everything away. This is a fair trade and equal exchange.

s.p: It is if it's true, but does require some trust. Yet you say God cannot put something in our hand, if we are already holding something else?

m.e: In order to educate and warn us, he often takes from us both physical and spiritual belongings, for the possession of honour should be his and not ours. Furthermore, we should keep all things only as if they had been merely lent and not given to us, without any sense of possessiveness, whether it be our body or soul, our senses, faculties, worldly goods or honour, friends, relations, house or home or anything whatsoever.

s.p: So if that's our intention in all this – what's God's intention?

m.e: It is that he wishes to be our sole possession. This is what he wills and intends. He strives for one thing only, that he is our sole possession.

s.p: He doesn't want much!

m.e: But here lies his greatest bliss and delight! The more he can be this, the greater is his bliss and joy! For the more we are in possession of other things, the less he is our possession.

s.p: And the less our experience of bliss and joy.

m.e: The less love we have for all things, the more we possess him with all that he can do for us. Therefore when our Lord spoke the beatitudes, he put poverty of spirit at the top. If there were a single foundation upon which all goodness could be built, then it would have to include this.

S.P: So unlike what we might imagine, poverty of spirit is actually a recipe for happiness; a rather joyful state?

M.E: In return for keeping ourselves detached from things which are outside us, God wishes to give us for our own possession all that is in heaven, even heaven itself together with all its powers; indeed with everything which ever flowed from it and which all angels and saints enjoy, so that all this may be ours, far more than any *thing* has ever been ours.

And now I'm suddenly ferreting around inside my pockets for a piece of paper I always carry with me, on which are written some words of a female German mystic, Mechthild of Magdeburg, for they echo what Eckhart has just said. Having found the piece of paper, and ironed out some of the creases, I ask Eckhart if I might read him her imagined dialogue between God and the soul. 'Why not?' he says, and so I do:

Soul: What do you require, Lord?

God: You should be naked.

Soul: But Lord, what will happen to me then?

God: Lady Soul, you share my nature so far that nothing can come between you and me. No angel has ever been honoured to know for a single hour what is yours from eternity!

Eckhart nods his head.

S.P: Your words, Meister, remind me of hers.

M.E: In return for stripping myself of myself for his sake, God will be wholly my own possession. Nothing was ever my own as much as God will be mine, together with all that he is and all that he can do.

S.P: So this seems important: who is a truly poor person? I mean, how might we recognize them; what would they look like?

M.E: They are truly poor in spirit who can easily do without everything which is not strictly necessary. That is why the man who sat naked in his tub, said to Alexander the Great, who ruled the whole world: 'I am greater than you are, for I have spurned more than you have seized. What you think is a great thing to possess, is too trivial for me to scorn!' They who can go without all things, not requiring them, are far more blessed than those who possess them in their need.

S.P: That does rather re-write the rules for greatness.

M.E: St Augustine said: 'Lord, I did not wish to lose you, but in my greed I wanted to have creatures as well as you, and thus I lost you for you do not allow us to possess the falsity and deception of creatures together with you, who are truth.'

S.P: I'm being reminded here of that old saying that our being attracts life; that what we *are* creates the life around us, for good or ill. Like attracts like.

M.E: All predilection, attachment and affection come from what is similar to us, since all things incline to and like what is the same as themselves. So a pure person likes all purity, and a just person likes and inclines to justice. And so it is a clear sign that it is creatures and not God which lives in our hearts, if we incline to external things and find comfort in them. Therefore a good man or woman should be ashamed before

God and themselves if they realize that God is not in us, but that it is rather wretched creatures that act within us, living in us and determining our affections. For an inclination towards external things; the finding of comfort in what is comfortless – and delight in much talk about these things – are a clear sign that God is not manifest in us and that he is neither alert nor active in us.

s.p: As I understand you, a poor person is a person who is naturally receptive to God; who can't help but receive God, because like attracts like. So tell me more about this poor person, because they seem rather important.

m.e: A poor person is someone who desires nothing, knows nothing and possesses nothing. It is of these three things I wish to speak, and I beseech you for the love of God to understand me if you can.

I feel the passion in his eyes; he cares about these things.

s.p: I'll do my best.

m.e: But if you do not understand then do not worry, for I shall be speaking of a particular kind of truth which only a few good people can grasp.

s.p: I'll remember that.

m.e: In the first place, then, a poor person is someone who desires nothing.

s.p: As you've said.

m.e: Now, some people do not understand this point correctly. I mean those who cling to their own egos in their penances and external devotions, which such people regard as being of great importance. God have mercy on them, for they know little of the divine truth! These people are called holy because of what they are seen to do, but inside they are asses! – for they do not know the real meaning of divine truth.

s.p: That's rather harsh.

m.e: These people are all right, for they mean well, and that is why they deserve our praise. May God in his mercy grant them heaven! But I tell you by the divine truth that such people are not truly poor, nor are they like those who are poor. They are greatly esteemed by people who know no better, of course. But I tell you that they are asses, who understand nothing of God's truth. May they attain heaven because of their good intent, but of that poverty, of which we now speak, they know nothing.

s.p: I'll be careful who I listen to. But tell me – what does it mean to desire nothing?

m.e: As long as it is someone's will to carry out the most precious will of God, such a person does not have that poverty of which I wish to speak.

s.p: Why not?

m.e: For this person still has a will with which they wish to please God, and this is not true poverty. If we are to have true poverty, then we must be free of our own created will just as we were before we were created. I tell you by the eternal truth that as long as you have the will to perform God's will, and a desire for eternity and for God – you are not yet poor! They alone are poor who will nothing and desire nothing. If we are to be poor in will, then we must will and desire as little as we willed and desired before we came into being. It is in this way that someone is poor who wills nothing.

S.P: And to know nothing?

M.E: They who are to have this particular poverty must live in such a way that they do not know that they do not live either for themselves, for truth or for God. Rather, they must be free of the knowledge that they do not know, understand or sense that God lives in them. And more even than this: they must be free of all knowledge that lives in them. For when we were contained within the eternal essence of God, there was nothing other than God in us! Therefore I say that we should be as free of self-knowledge as we were before we were created; that we should allow God to do what he will and that we should be entirely free of all things. This is why it is necessary that we should desire to know or perceive nothing of God's works. In this way we can become poor in knowing.

S.P: And so to the third kind of poverty. You did say there were three sorts. A poverty of desiring; a poverty of knowing and –

M.E: – the third kind of poverty is the ultimate one, and this is the poverty of someone who possesses nothing. We should be so poor that we neither are, nor possess, a place in which God can act.

S.P: Well, now you've surprised me again. Because surely we should all have such a place; a place where God can work?

M.E: Not at all. If we still have such a place within us, then we still have multiplicity. And so it is that I ask God to make me free of 'God' – for my most essential being is above 'God', in so far as we conceive of God as the origin of creatures. And so in that essence, where God is above all existence and all multiplicity: I myself was there –

S.P: – before creation?

M.E: There I desired myself and knew myself to make this man. Therefore I am my own self cause, according to my essence, which is eternal; and not according to my becoming, which is in time. There I am unborn, and according to the manner of my unbornness, I shall never die. There I am above all creatures and am neither 'God' nor creature, but I am rather what I once was and what I shall remain now and forever more. God can find no place in us then, for with this poverty we attain that which we have eternally been and shall forever remain. Here God is one with our spirit, and this is poverty in its ultimate form.

S.P: So what you say is this: that though on one level we are trapped in time, on another level, we can return inwardly to our pre-existent form, when we were one with all things, and free of the multiplicity of form and image which we know now; a time when we were without even the images of God we know now. These are hard words to understand.

M.E: Whoever does not understand these words should not be troubled. For as long as someone is not in themselves akin to this truth, they will not understand my words, since this is an unconcealed truth which came directly from the heart of God.

S.P: The Dominican tradition is to pass on to others, what you have received in meditation. I sense that is what is happening here. So just confirm this for us – you say it is all right to know nothing? For many, it might seem like a lack.

M.E: Your unknowing is not a lack but rather, your highest perfection, and passively to receive is your highest action.

S.P: That's clear enough.

M.E: In this way you must cease being active and must draw all your powers to a point of stillness, if you truly desire to experience the birth of God within yourself. If you wish to find the new-born king, then you must ignore everything which you might otherwise find, and cast it aside.

s.p: OK. But what is there then left for my reason to do? Can I unknow the things I know? Should I stand in complete darkness?

m.e: Yes indeed! You are never better placed than when you are in complete darkness and unknowing.

s.p: But must it all be removed? Can there be no return to my former self?

m.e: No, truly; there can be no return.

s.p: So no return to my former self as I enter this darkness. Then tell us more about this darkness we must enter. What does the word 'darkness' describe?

m.e: Its name means nothing other than a state of potential receptivity. And if you were to ask how beneficial it is to pursue this potentiality and to maintain ourselves in bareness and simplicity, holding only to this darkness and unknowing, without turning back – then I would say that it offers the sole possibility of gaining him who is all things. The more you are empty of self and freed from the knowledge of objects, the closer you come to him. Concerning this desert, Hosea writes: 'I will lead my beloved into the wilderness and will speak to her in her heart.'

s.p: But won't we be driven mad by the dark wilderness? Shouldn't we at least do something like pray or read or some other virtuous action in order to help ourselves survive?

m.e: You cannot turn away from this state to other things

without doing yourself harm, that much is sure. You wish to be prepared in part by yourself, and in part by God, which cannot be. You yourself cannot think about or desire this preparation more swiftly than God can carry it out. But supposing that it could be divided: the preparation would then be yours, and the in-pouring or action would be his, which is quite impossible. You should know that God must pour himself into you and act upon you where he finds you prepared. You should not think that God is like a carpenter on earth who works or does not work as he will, and for whom it is a matter of choice as to whether he should do something or not, according to his inclination. This is not the case with God who must act and must pour himself into you wherever and whenever he finds you prepared, just as the sun must pour itself forth and cannot hold itself back when the air is pure and clean. Certainly it would be a major failing if God did not perform great works in you, pouring great goodness into you, in so far as he finds you empty and bare.

Again, Eckhart here echoes Mechthild, who also said that God must act; that it was in his nature to do so, when the circumstances were right.

s.p: So we do not seek God?

m.e: You need not seek him either here nor there, for he is no further than the door of your heart. There he stands, waiting for someone who is ready to open the door and let him in. You do not need to call him from far away; he can hardly wait for you to let him in. The opening of the door and his entering in, happen in exactly the same moment.

s.p: Some will say: how is this so? They will say they cannot feel God's presence in this way; that it is simply not always like that.

M.E: Listen to this. Sensing his presence is not in your power but in his. He will show himself when it suits him to do so, and he can also stay hidden if that is his wish. This is what Christ meant when he said to Nicodemus: 'The spirit breathes where it will: you hear its voice but do not know where it comes from or where it is going.'

S.P: But whether we feel it or not, in a state of receptivity, we cannot help but receive?

M.E: In everything that you see or hear, whatever it may be, in all things you can receive nothing but his birth. All things become pure God to you, for in all things you see nothing but God.

S.P: Does someone who is spiritually advanced in this way still need to practice the disciplines of devotion – or are they beyond such things?

M.E: Listen to this! All forms of penance – fasting, vigils, prayer, kneeling, self-flagellation, hair shirts, sleeping on boards or whatever – were created because the body and the flesh are always opposed to the spirit. The body is often too strong for it, and there is constant warfare between them, an eternal struggle. Here on earth, it is the body which is bold and strong, for it feels at home. The world aids it, and all its serving-maids support it: food, drink and physical comfort – but all these work against the spirit. And so here on earth, the soul is in exile: all her serving-maids and relatives are in heaven. There she is well connected, if she establishes herself there, and makes herself at home.

S.P: So penitential practice is to redress the balance of power?

M.E: Indeed. It is in order to assist the spirit here in exile and to weaken the flesh in this struggle, that we restrain it with penitential practices; curbing it so the spirit can resist it. This is done in order to constrain the flesh, but believe me, if you lay upon it the bridle of love, then you will tame and constrain it in a way that is a thousand times better. Nothing brings you closer to God and gives you God so much as this sweet bond of love.

s.p: Though we've been talking about detachment, it has almost become a meditation on unknowing.

m.e: Though it may be called a nescience, an unknowing, there is within it, more than all knowing and understanding without it; for this unknowing lures and attracts you from all understood things; and from yourself as well.

s.p: Meister Eckhart, for the moment, thank you. We will continue our discussion after Terce.

TWO

The spiritual life

Little is known of Eckhart's early life, beyond that he was born into a wealthy family, in Tambach south of Gotha in Thuringia in 1260. The next recorded fact is that he joined the Dominican Order, or The Order of Preachers, at the age of 15.

This order had been founded by St Dominic, in 1215, to combat heresy; and was famous for its intellectual tradition. By the time of Eckhart, however, and in response to changing times, it was more open to the contemplative and mystical elements of spirituality, whilst retaining its academic roots. One of its earliest battles had been with the Albigensians in the South of France. These people believed that all matter was evil, and that only spirit was good. This belief threatened Roman Catholic views on the incarnation of Christ, and they were savagely persecuted. If all matter was bad, then Christ was bad.

But sometimes, as I listened to Eckhart stressing the supreme value of the soul at the expense of material things, I wondered if he showed similar tendencies to the Albigensians. Perhaps I'd learn more as we discussed the spiritual life in our next session. I was certainly interested to hear what he had to say about this. I knew he distrusted rigid spiritual programmes, as he did not believe there was a single way to God to be trod by all. But did he have any practical suggestions as to the steps we might take? After all, he'd looked after enough novices in his time, guiding them in their spiritual lives. So could he give me a method for spiritual progress? I suspected he might, for as one of his students intriguingly told me, 'The usefulness of Meister Eckhart is not always appreciated.'

The cool of the early morning is beginning to give way to a warming breeze, as we settle again in the north cloister.

s.p: So, to start us off, Meister Eckhart, some pastoral advice, please, for anyone feeling a little insecure or battered today. What should they do?

m.e: Do exactly what they would do if they felt secure.

s.p: And that's it?

m.e: That's enough. Do exactly what you would do if you felt secure.

s.p: I like it. And I can guess your reason for this sense of security.

m.e: Whoever has God as a companion is with him in all places, both on the street and among people, as well as in church or in the desert or in a monastic cell.

s.p: How is this so?

m.e: It is so because such a person possesses God alone, keeping their gaze fixed on God, and thus all things become God for him or her. Such people bear God in all their deeds and in all the places they go, and it is God alone who is author of all their deeds. If we keep our eyes fixed on God alone, then truly he must work in us; and nothing, neither the crowd, nor any place, can hinder him in this. And so nothing will be able to hinder us, if we desire and seek God alone, and take pleasure in nothing else. We must learn to maintain our inner solitude regardless of where we are or who we are with.

This seemed a helpful pointer in the spiritual life. But did it require any particular practice I wondered. Or did I have to work that out for myself?

s.p: So what spiritual practice does God ask of me?

M.E: God expects but one thing of you, and that is that you should come out of yourself in so far as you are a created being made, and let be God be God in you.

S.P: I think often it is my mind which is busy being me; and probably isn't me at all.

M.E: You must know that God is born in us when the mind is stilled and sense troubles us no longer. All things become simply God to you, for in all things you notice only God.

S.P: So God won't fit around my schedule?

M.E: Light and darkness are incompatible, like God and creatures. Enter God, exit creatures. Man is quite conscious of this light. Directly he turns to God, this light begins to glint and sparkle in him, telling him what to do and what to leave undone, accompanied by many a shrewd hint of things he has previously ignored and known nothing of.

S.P: So God is like a light in us, guiding. But how do we know what is of the light and what isn't? Even the Inquisition imagines it fights for the light.

M.E: God attracts you to God and you are aware of many a virtuous impulse, albeit uncertain whence it comes. This interior mood is in no way due to creatures, for what creatures effect and direct comes in from outside. But your inner self is stirred by this force, and the freer you keep yourself, the more truth and discernment are yours.

S.P: Things often come back to discernment, I find!

M.E: No man was ever lost save for the reason that once having left his inner ground, he has let himself become too permanently settled abroad. The truth is within his own ground; not beyond it. So he who is determined to see this light and find out the whole truth, must foster the awareness of this birth within himself, in his own ground. In this manner will his powers be lit, and his outer being as well. As soon as God inwardly stirs his ground with the truth, its light darts into his powers, and lo and behold, that man knows more than anyone could teach him!

s.p: Anyone? Even the wisest teacher?

m.e: Of course. As the prophet says, 'I know more than I was ever taught.'

s.p: So what about all your wonderful Dominican libraries?

m.e: A master of life is worth more than a thousand masters of books.

s.p: So going back a little – you're saying that light does not come to me via my gifts? The world may applaud them, but they can never be the place where God's truth is lit in me?

m.e: This inner birth is inconsistent with darkness and sin, and occurs not in the powers, but in the ground and essence of the soul.

s.p: You don't spell it out, but obedience seems very important in your teaching about the spiritual life.

m.e: True and perfect obedience is a virtue above all virtues, and there is no work, however great it may be, that can take place or be performed without this virtue, and even the very least of works, whether it be saying or listening to Mass, praying, meditating or whatever you can think of, is more usefully done when it is performed in true obedience.

s.p: Carry on.

m.e: Take any work you can think of and however small it may be, true obedience will make it nobler and better for you. Obedience brings out the very best in all things, and never neglects what is good. And obedience need never be anxious – for there is no form of goodness which it does not possess in itself.

s.p: So obedience become happiness?

m.e: When we go out of ourselves through obedience, and strip ourselves of what is ours, then God must enter into us; for when someone wills nothing for themselves, then God must will on their behalf just as he does for himself. Whenever I have taken leave of my own will, putting it in the hands of my superior, and no longer will anything for myself, then God must will on my behalf, and if he neglects me in this respect, then he neglects himself. And so in all things in which I do not will for myself, God wills on my behalf.

s.p: I can understand that. But what if I myself want or will something to happen? I probably do this five times before breakfast.

m.e: In true obedience, there should be no 'I want this to happen or that to happen' or 'I want this or that thing' – but only a pure going out of what is our own. And therefore in the very best kind of prayer, there should be no 'give me this particular virtue or way of devotion,' but rather, 'Lord, give me only what you will, and in the way that you will.' This kind of prayer is as far above the former, as heaven is above earth. And when we have prayed in this way, then we have prayed well, having gone out of ourselves and entered God in true obedience. And just as true obedience should have no 'I want this' in it, neither should it hear 'I don't want', either; for 'I don't want' is pure poison for all true obedience.

s.p: Then what is the most powerful form of prayer, if it is not to ask for what we want?

m.e: The most powerful form of prayer, and the one which can gain almost all things and which is the worthiest work of all, is that which flows from a free mind. The freer the mind is, the more powerful and worthy; the more useful, praiseworthy and perfect prayer and work become. A free mind can achieve all things.

s.p: That's very quotable. And a free mind can achieve all things, because it is not tied to any particular outcome?

m.e: A free mind is one that is quite untroubled and unfettered by anything; which has not tied itself to any way of being or devotion, and does not seek its own interest in anything. Rather, it is forever immersed in God's most precious will, having left its own. There is no work which men and women can perform, however small, which does not draw from this leaving its power and its strength.

s.p: So prayer strengthens us?

m.e: We should pray with such intensity that we want all the members of our body and all its faculties – eyes, ears mouth, heart and all our senses – to turn to this end; and we should not cease in this until we feel that we are close to being united with him who is present to us, and to whom we are praying: God.

s.p: Would this be easier if we all withdrew from the world and became hermits?

m.e: No. The person who is in the right state of mind is so, regardless of where they are and who they are with. While those who are in the wrong state of mind will find this to be the case wherever they are, and who ever they are with. Those who intend and seek only God, nothing can obstruct these people; for they are united with God in all their aims. And so, just as no multiplicity can divide God, in the same way, nothing scatters or divides a person such as this, for they are one in the One in whom all multiplicity is one, and who is non-multiplicity.

s.p: So the good mind is the single mind, rather than the distracted mind. The distracted mind loves different options as it approaches God. The single mind knows only inner oneness.

m.e: Those who must constantly receive God in one external thing after another, seeking God in diverse ways – whether in particular works, people or places – well, such a person does not possess God. The least thing can impede them, for they neither have God and nor do they seek, love and intend him alone.

s.p: They want add-ons?

m.e: And so it is that both bad company and good company give them problems; both the street and the church; both evil words and deeds and good words and deeds – for the obstruction lies within themselves, since in them God has not become all things.

s.p: So how can God become all things within us?

m.e: The real possession of God is to be found in the heart; in an inner movement of the spirit towards him and striving for him, and not just in thinking about him always and in the same way. We should not content ourselves with a God of thoughts – for when the thoughts come to an end, so too shall our God! Rather, we should have a living God who is beyond the thoughts of all people and all creatures. That kind of God will not leave us, unless we ourselves choose to turn away from him.

s.p: To possess God in our being, rather than in our thoughts? That is an inspiring vision.

m.e: Whoever possesses God in their being possesses him in a divine manner, and he shines out to them in all things; for them, all things taste of God, and in all things it is only God's image they see. God is radiant in them; inwardly, they are detached from the world, and inwardly formed by the loving presence of their God. Compare it to someone with a great thirst. Although they may be doing something other than drinking with their minds turned to other things, the thought of a drink will not leave them for as long as they thirst. Whatever they do, whoever they are with, whatever they strive for – the greater and more intense becomes the thought of a drink.

We should be similarly permeated with a sense of the divine presence and be inwardly formed with the form of our beloved God; be so established in him that we see his presence effortlessly, and more than this, remain unencumbered by anything and free of all things. But this will initially demand from us as much application and concentration, as any art form does when one attempts to learn it.

s.p: The sun may be out, and this cloister most peaceful – but I must confess to feeling a little deflated. I thought I was doing rather well in the spiritual life before meeting you.

m.e: No one should ever judge what they do positively, or as having been done so well that they become so casual or self-confident in their actions that their reason grows lazy or slumbers.

s.p: Point taken.

m.e: But they should always elevate themselves with the twin faculties of reason and will, thus activating the very best in them selves; and protecting them selves against all harm by means of understanding in matters both internal and external. Thus they will not fail in anything anywhere but will make constant spiritual progress.

s.p: So it is not about judging our personal performance; but about looking at what it is that we will.

m.e: Nothing should terrify us as long as we will the good; and nor should we be depressed if we cannot fulfil our will in what we do. In that case, we should not regard ourselves as being far from virtues, for virtue and all that is good live in a good will. And what you desire with your whole will, that is your possession, and neither God nor any creature can take it from you; as long as your will is undivided and is a truly godly will, fixed in the present moment.

s.p: The temptation is to think I can do it later.

m.e: Do not say: 'I should like to do it later,' which would refer to the future, but rather, 'I wish it to be so now.' Note this: when I want something even if it is a thousand miles away, then it is more truly mine than something in my lap which I do not want to have.

s.p: The will is a powerful tool, I agree; especially if the will has a cause. Then, as I have witnessed, anything can be done and endured without complaint.

m.e: This is so. It is a natural truth that when someone undertakes a task with some other purpose in mind, then the final goal for the sake of which they undertake the work is more precious to them, whilst their labour is less important – affecting them only with respect to the cause that drives them on. He who builds – cutting wood and dressing stone in order to erect a house which will stand against the summer heat and winter cold – this person has his heart set first and foremost on the house, and would never chisel a stone and get down to the work if it wasn't for the sake of the house. And the same is true, although to an incomparably higher degree, when someone performs all their works for the sake of God.

s.p: OK. But how do we know when such deeds are performed for the sake of God? In other words, how do we know when our will is a right will?

m.e: The will is perfect and right when it has no selfhood and when it has left itself, having been taken up and transformed into the will of God. Truly, the more this is so, the more it is right and true. And with such a will you can achieve all things, whether this be love or whatever it is that you wish.

s.p: But other people seem to perform much greater works than me. This is how I feel. They all seem much more loving.

m.e: There are two things you must consider here, my friend: the first is the essence of love, and the second is the work or the outflow of love. Love resides essentially in the will alone, so whoever has more will, has more of love.

s.p: I haven't heard it put in that manner before.

m.e: But there is something else, and that is the outflow or work of love. On the face of it, this is easily visible as inwardness and devotion and celebration. Such is not always the best way, however, for it is possible these things arise not from love at all, but that is nature giving people an experience of sweetness and delight; or perhaps heaven's influence or something conveyed by the senses. Suffice to say, those who experience such things most frequently are not necessarily the best people.

s.p: So spiritual ecstasy and visions are not important signs of health?

m.e: No. And as such people grow in love, it may well be that they have less sense and awareness of it. And only then it can be seen whether they truly possess love; by the extent to which they remain wholly faithful to God without heightened feelings of this kind.

s.p: So let me catch breath: you're saying that those who have special spiritual experiences are not necessarily the most loving people; that love is more about the will than being caught up in some seventh heaven; and that the test comes when the ecstatic experiences dry up?

m.e: You must sometimes leave your state of exaltation for the sake of something better out of love; to perform an act of love where this is needed, either spiritually or physically. For instance, If you knew of a sick person who needed a bowl of soup from you, then I would consider it far better for you to leave your ecstasy for the sake of love and to administer to the needy person in a love that is greater.

s.p: I can see that. I suppose we seek heightened spiritual experiences because they give us consolation of some sort.

m.e: You should know that the friends of God are never without consolation, for their greatest consolation is what God wills for them, whether it be for their comfort or not.

s.p: And that requires much trust, as I think you're aware.

Meister Eckhart smiles a mischievous smile.

M.E: We recognize true and perfect love by whether or not someone has great hope and confidence in God; for there is nothing which testifies more clearly to perfect love than trust. Wholehearted love for another creates trust in them, and we will truly find in God everything that we dare hope for in him – and a thousand times more. Just as we can never love God too much, neither can we have too much trust in him. Nothing we may ever do can ever be so appropriate as fully trusting God.

S.P: But you must know, Meister, that God can sometimes feel very distant and not at all easy to find.

M.E: You should know that a good will cannot fail to find God, even though the mind sometimes feels that it misses him; and indeed often believes that he has departed altogether! What should you do then? Do exactly the same as you would if you were experiencing the greatest consolation –

S.P: Do exactly what you would do if you felt secure –

M.E: Learn to do the same in the greatest suffering, and behave in exactly the same way as you did in consolation. There is no better advice on how to find God than to seek him where we left him; do now what you did when you last had him, and then you will find him again. But in truth, a good will can never lose God or fail to find him.

S.P: I suspect most of us believe our will is good.

M.E: Many people say that their will is good when they do not have God's will at all, but wish to keep their own will and instruct the Lord to do this and that! Although St Paul spoke at length with our Lord and our Lord with him, this helped him not at all until he gave up his own will and said: 'Lord, what is it you wish me to do?' And it was just the same when the angel appeared to Mary: nothing which they said to each other could have made her the mother of God. But as soon as she gave up her will, and left herself, she immediately became a true mother of the Eternal Word and conceived God straight away. And nothing makes us true so much as giving up our will. Indeed, just suppose we went so far as to give up the whole of our will, daring to abandon all things for God's sake, both inner and outer – well, then we would have accomplished everything. But not before.

s.p: Take leave of ourselves?

m.e: Put it like this: if someone were to leave themselves entirely, then truly they would be so rooted in God that if anyone were to touch them, they would first have to touch God. They would be wrapped in God, as my head is wrapped in my hood – so that if anyone wants to touch me, they must first touch my clothing. And however great your suffering may be, if it first passes through God, then he must be the first to endure it. Indeed, in the truth which God is, no suffering which befalls us is so small, whether discomfort or inconvenience, that it does not touch God infinitely more than ourselves; and does not happen to him more than to us, in so far as we place it in God. But if God endures it for the sake of the benefit for you which he has foreseen in it; and if you are willing to suffer what he suffers and what passes through him to you – then the experience takes on the colour of God, and shame becomes honour; bitterness is sweet and the deepest darkness becomes the clearest light! Then everything takes its flavour from God, and becomes divine. Thus we shall grasp God in all bitterness as well as in the greatest sweetness.

s.p: So light and darkness are but one and the same for those who know God. But what do we do with sin? Can even this become sweet?

M.E: It is not being tempted to sin which is sinful; but consenting to sin; it is wanting to lose your temper which is sinful. Virtue, like vice, is a matter of the will.

S.P: And yet we do often will it.

M.E: Truly, to commit a sin is not sinful if we regret what we've done. God is a God of the present. He takes you and receives you as he finds you now, not as you have been, but as you are now. God willingly endures all the harm and shame which all our sins have inflicted upon him, as he has done for many years, in order that we should come to a deep knowledge of his love and in order that our love and our gratitude should increase and our zeal grow more intense, which often happens when we have repented of our sins.

S.P: I'm not always sure if I've repented or not. I may regret something, but that is not quite the same. Regret just makes me unhappy.

M.E: There are two types of repentance. One type draws us spiralling downwards into yet greater suffering; plunging us into such distress that it is as if we were already in a state of despair. This repentance finds no way out of suffering, and nothing comes of it.

But repentance which is of God is very different. As soon as we become ill at ease, we immediately reach up to God and vow with an unshakeable will to turn away from all sin forever. Thus we raise ourselves up to a great trust in God and gain a great sense of certainty.

S.P: So true penance is not beating our selves with a stick?

M.E: Many people believe they are achieving great things in external works such as fasting, going barefoot and other such practices which are called penances. But true penance consists in turning entirely away from all that is not God or of God, and in turning fully and completely towards our beloved God in unshakeable love, so that our devotion and desire for him become great. If any external work hampers you in this – whether it's fasting, keeping vigil, reading or whatever else – you should freely let it go, without any worry that you might thereby be neglecting your penance. God does not notice the nature of the works themselves; only the love, devotion and spirit that is in them. For he is not so much concerned with our works as with the spirit with which we perform them all.

S.P: So it is we who distance ourselves from God by our spirit?

M.E: If your great sins have ever driven you so far from him that you regard yourself as not being close to God, then you should still regard God as being close to you. It can be very destructive if we regard God as being distant from us, since whether we are far from him or near to him, he is never far from us and always close at hand. If for some reason he cannot remain within, then he goes no further than the door.

At that moment, the monastery gates creak open as the beer delivery enters the court yard. There is a little noise, but Eckhart does not appear distracted. And I'm now thinking about his work as a spiritual counsellor, when presumably no two people are the same; or wish to be treated as the same.

S.P: I notice that you are hesitant to prescribe any particular way in the spiritual life. You speak of attitude, but don't say we should do this, or that or the other. Does this mean we have to find our own way?

M.E: People should remember that if they see a good person

who is following a way which is different from theirs, then they are wrong to think that such a person's efforts are all in vain. If someone else's way of devotion gives them problems, then they are ignoring the goodness in it as well as the person's good intention, and this is unhelpful. It is best that we see the true feeling in people's devotional practices and not scorn the particular way anyone follows. Not everyone can follow the same way, nor can all people follow only one way; and nor can we follow all the different ways or everyone else's way!

s.p: Well, that's true. It would all get very exhausting, mimicking other people's devotions.

m.e: Indeed. So you should not confine yourself to just one manner of devotion, since God is to be found in no particular way, neither this way nor that way. That is why they do him wrong who take God in just one particular way. They take the way rather than God. Intend God alone, and seek him only. Then whatever kinds of devotional practice come to you, be content with those. For your intention should be directed at God alone and nothing else. Then what you like and dislike is all right, and you should know that to do it differently is to do it wrongly.

s.p: There is much 'faddery' in spirituality; the latest good idea. A new voice appears, and everyone says 'This is it!' Next year it will be something else, of course.

m.e: They who desire so many ways of devotion push God under a bench. Whether it is the gift of tears or sighings or the like – none of this is God. If these come to you, all well and good; if they do not come to you, that too is all right.

s.p: I suppose when choosing our devotions, the church usually says we should follow Jesus' way.

M.E: Our Lord fasted for forty days but no one should attempt to imitate him in this. As I have often said: I regard the work of the spirit as being far better than the work of the body.

S.P: But how does this work out in practice? If we don't follow Christ precisely, what do we do?

M.E: Christ fasted for 40 days. You should follow him in this by considering what it is which you are most inclined or ready to do; and then you should give it up, while observing yourself closely. Sometimes it is more difficult to refrain from uttering one word, than it is to refrain from speaking altogether. And it is far more difficult being solitary in a crowd than it is being alone in the desert.

S.P: So it's about observing ourselves in order to understand our particular compulsions; those things we are most inclined to do. Of course, some of us may not wish to discover these things!

M.E: Willingly discover all things from God, and follow him, and all will be well with you. Then you will be able to accept honour and comfort; and if dishonour and discomfort were to be your lot, you could and would be just as willing to endure these too. They can justifiably feast who would be just as willingly fast.

S.P: I'm aware that I fall far short of that vision; yet do feel my heart to be in the right place. So why do I struggle? Does it have to be so hard?

M.E: God, who is faithful remember, allows his friends to fall frequently into weakness only to remove from them any false prop on which they might lean; for he desires to give them great gifts, solely and only on account of his goodness.

And he shall be their comfort and support while they discover themselves to be a pure nothingness in all the great gifts of God. The more essentially and simply the mind rests on God, the more receptive we are to him in all his precious gifts; for human kind should build on God alone.

S.P: I know some who have felt so estranged from God they're quite unable to take the bread and the wine.

M.E: Whoever wants to receive the body of our Lord does not need to scrutinize what they are feeling at the time; or how great their piety or devotion is. Rather, they should notice the state of their will and attitude of mind. You should not place too much weight on your feelings, but emphasize rather the object of your love and striving.

S.P: So it's will above feelings; I can see that's wise. But even so, what if I feel too empty and cold to go to our Lord – let alone speak of love for him?

M.E: Then the greater is your need to go to your God, for he shall inflame you and make you burn with zeal! –

S.P: – Like a cold fire reawakened? –

M.E: – And in him you shall be sanctified, joined and made one with him alone. Only in the sacrament and nowhere else shall you truly find that your mind and all your scattered senses – previously separated from each other and too inclined to tend downwards – are now united, gathered up together, and properly offered to God. Thus you shall be united with him and made noble through his body. Indeed, in the body of our Lord, the soul is so united with God that none of the angels can distinguish or discover a difference between them; for where they touch God they touch the soul; and where they touch the soul, they touch God! There has never been

such an absolute union, for the union of the soul with God,
is far closer than that of the body and the soul, which creates
a person. And let me tell you – this union is far closer than
when someone pours a drop of water into a barrel of wine;
the latter would be water and wine, whereas the former are so
united with each other that no creature in heaven or earth can
find a difference between them!

s.p: A union such as that is almost beyond imagining; and
sounds wonderful as you speak it. But in the daily routine of
life, these higher things are not always on my mind.

m.e: Beware of two things about yourself which were also
true of our Lord. He too had higher and lower faculties and
their respective functions were different. His higher faculties
enjoyed eternal blessedness while at the same time his lower
faculties found themselves in the greatest suffering and
struggle on earth, and neither of these two interfered with each
other. In you too the higher faculties should be raised to God,
offered up to him and united with him. Indeed, we should
assign all suffering to the body, the lower faculties and the
senses; whereas the spirit should rise up with all its power and
immerse itself freely in its God.

s.p: We are to call on our higher self to keep us inwardly free,
whatever our circumstances?

m.e: Staying inwardly free requires rigorous commitment
and two things in particular. The first is that we seal ourselves
off internally, so that our minds are protected from external
images which therefore remain outside and do not unfittingly
associate with us or keep our company or find a place to lodge
in us.

s.p: Right. And the second way of staying inwardly free?

M.E: The second is that neither in our inner images, whether these be representations of things or sublime thoughts, nor in external images or whatever happens to be present to us, should we allow ourselves to be dissipated or scattered or externalized through multiplicity. We should apply and train all our faculties to this end, maintaining our inwardness. For the inward person, of course, even external things possess an inward and divine manner of being.

S.P: This is work which requires discipline.

M.E: When the understanding is corrupted in a young person, or in anyone at all, then it must be trained again with much effort. For however much it may enjoy a natural affinity with God, as soon as it is wrongly directed and becomes fixed on things created, growing used to them and becoming swamped with their images, then it becomes weak in this part and dispossessed of itself and hindered in its noble striving. Once we have weaned ourselves from such things and distanced ourselves from them, we can begin to act wisely, freely delighting in each act or choosing against it. Further, if there is something we like and enjoy and which we indulge in with the assent of our will, whether it is something we eat or drink or whatever it may be – then this is something an unpractised person cannot do without being damaged in some way.

S.P: But it's work, work, *work?*

M.E: No. A man should strive with the divine presence without having to work for it. He should get the essence out of things and let the things themselves alone. That requires at first attentiveness and exact impressions, as with the student and his art. So the soul must be permeated with the divine presence, and inwardly formed with the form of the beloved God who is within her, so that she may radiate the presence of God without working at it.

S.P: What I hear is that we are not all at the same level of awareness or possibility; that we need to learn how to handle the different gifts given to us.

M.E: We must train ourselves not to seek or strive for our own interests in anything, but rather to find and grasp God in all things. For God does not give us anything in order that we should enjoy its possession and rest content with it; nor has he ever done so. All the gifts he has ever granted us in heaven or on earth were made solely in order to be able to give us the *one* gift, which is him self. For there can be no attachment to a particular way of behaving in this life, nor has this ever been right, however successful we may have been. Above all, we should always focus on the gifts of God, and always do so afresh. For instance, I know of someone who greatly desired something from our Lord, but I told her that she was simply not properly prepared and that if God gave her the gift in this unprepared state, it would then be lost.

S.P: Gifts need careful handling?

M.E: If we are not ready for it, the gift will be spoiled and God with the gift. That is why also God cannot always give what we ask for. We do violence to him and wrong by obstructing him in his natural work, through being unprepared. We must learn to free ourselves from all our gifts, not holding on to what is our own or seeking anything – either profit, pleasure, inwardness, sweetness, reward, heaven or our own will. God never gives himself, or ever has given himself, to a will that is alien to himself, but only to his own will.

S.P: Like attracts like.

M.E: Where he finds his own will, he gives himself and enters in with all that he is. Thus it is not enough to give ourselves up just the once, together with all that we have and are capable of.

Rather, we must renew ourselves constantly, thus maintaining our freedom and simplicity in all things.

s.p: So we constantly start afresh. We get up each morning and start afresh. How should we do this?

m.e: Whoever wishes to start a new life or work, should turn to their God, desiring with all their strength and devotion that he should give them that which is best; that which is most precious to him and honourable. While they desire and intend nothing for themselves except the most precious will of God and that alone. They should then accept what God gives them as being directly from him, holding it to be quite the best thing of all; and wholly content with it.

s.p: I sense here that the essence of the spiritual life is the call to leave our distracted lives, and focus.

m.e: We should only ever do the one thing, since we cannot do all things. We best choose the single way, and in that way make all things our own. For if we determined to do all things, this and that, abandoning our own path for another which seems for a moment more favourable, then this would lead to great instability. We should not start one thing today and another thing tomorrow worrying that we might miss out on something. With God, we can miss out on nothing. We can no more miss anything with God, than God can. Accept the one way from God, and draw all that is good into it. And if it turns out that two things that you do are not compatible, this is a clear sign they are not from God. As Jesus said, 'A kingdom divided against itself will not stand.'

s.p: Yet you wish also for us a balance between our inner and outer works. You want us to *do* good, as well as *be* good. So how is this done? Must we abandon our inner life to take an active role in the world?

M.E: It is not that we should abandon, neglect or deny our inner self, but rather, learn to work precisely in it, with it and from it in such a way that inwardness leads to effective action and effective action takes us back to inwardness; and so we become used to acting without any compulsion. We should concentrate on the inner prompting, and act from it; but if external activity destroys the inner life, then give priority to the latter. Of course, if both are united as one, then that is best for cooperating with God.

S.P: That's helpful. And in the meantime, other people are none of my business? When I am feeling low, I tend to imagine they have everything I don't; and suffer accordingly.

M.E: No, do not be concerned either with the nature or the manner which God has given someone else. If I were reckoned good enough and holy enough to be considered among the saints, then people would discuss and question whether this was by grace or nature and be troubled by it. But this would be wrong of them. Let God work in you, acknowledge that it is his work, and do not be concerned about whether he achieves this by nature or by means beyond nature. Both nature and grace are his! So let him work how and where and in the way it suits him to do so.

Be like the man who wanted to channel a spring into his garden and said: 'I'm not concerned with the type of channel used, whether made of iron, wood, bone or rusty metal – as long as I get the water!' So just let God act, and be at peace. As far as you are in God, you are in peace; and as far as you are outside God, you are outside peace. Lack of peace comes from created things and not from God. Nor is there anything to fear in God, and nothing in him to cause sadness; his being can draw only love from us. It is true: they who have all they wish for, know joy; but no one has this except those whose will is one with God's will. May God grant us this union!

s.p: Indeed.

m.e: And note this: if it were possible to empty a cup completely and to keep it empty of anything that might fill it, free even of air; then without doubt, the cup would deny and forget its own nature – and be drawn up to heaven by its emptiness! In the same way, being naked and poor and empty of all created things draws the soul up to God. Likeness and warmth also draw us upwards.

s.p: Explain please.

m.e: Well, we have a visible analogy for this when material fire ignites wood, for then a spark takes on the nature of fire and becomes identical to the fire.

s.p: Like attracts like; warmth attracts warmth, and the two become one. Is this what you mean when you talk about the 'just person'? In that God is drawn to them, like to like, because of who they are?

m.e: The just man or woman lives in God, and God lives in them; for God must be born in the just, as they are in him, since every one of the just person's virtues gives birth to God and gives him delight. And not only every virtue of the just, but also every good work, however small, which is done through the just person and in justice, these too give God joy. Those who are slow of understanding should simply accept this; while those who are enlightened should know it.

s.p: I may be with the slow of understanding.

m.e: The just person seeks nothing through their works, for those whose works are aimed at a particular end or who act with a particular 'why' in view, are servants and hirelings. If you wish to be formed and transformed into justice then do not intend anything in particular by your works and do not embrace any particular agenda, neither in time nor eternity, neither reward nor blessedness, neither this nor that; such works in truth are dead. Indeed, even if you make God your goal, all the works you perform for his sake will be dead, and you will only spoil those works which are genuinely good. You will be like a gardener who is supposed to plant a garden but who pulls out all the trees instead, and then demands his wages. That is how you will spoil your good works. And so, if you wish to live and wish also for your works to live too, then be dead to all things and reduced to nothing. It is a characteristic of creatures to make one thing from another; but it is a characteristic of God to make something from nothing. And so if God is to make something of you or in you, then you must first yourself become nothingness. Enter your own inner ground, and act from there; and all your works shall be living works.

s.p: Thank you, because again, I find that helpfully put. But now, perhaps a more personal question, Meister. As we know, you've been defending yourself against all sorts of accusations over the past year. Over a hundred of your sayings have been condemned by the inquisition; while Herman de Summo and William de Nidecke, have been less than honourable witnesses for the prosecution. You must be glad of friends at a time like this.

m.e: If you love yourself, then you love everyone as much as yourself. But as long as there is someone who you do not love as much as yourself, then in truth, you have never properly loved yourself. A person who loves themselves and everyone as much as themselves is doing the best thing. Now some people say: I love my friend, who is a source of good things in my life, more than I do someone else. This is not right, though; it is imperfect. But we must accept it, just as some people cross the sea with a slack wind and still reach the other side. It is the same with those who love one person more than another; although this is natural enough. But if I loved him or her as much as I loved myself, I would be just as happy that whatever happens to them, whether joy or pain, death or life, should happen instead to me; and that would be true friendship.

s.p: Friendship with your self brings friendship with the world; and a friendship without strings. So are the perfect somehow beyond both joy and sorrow; untouched by either?

m.e: This is wrong.

s.p: Why is it wrong?

m.e: I tell you there can never be a saint who is so great that they cannot be moved in this way. I say rather that it may be given to a saint in this life that nothing can distract them from God.

s.p: But surely as long as words can move you to joy or sorrow you are imperfect!

m.e: This is not the case! And it was not true even for Christ himself. Christ was so hurt by words that if a single creature were to suffer the griefs of all, this would not be so terrible as the suffering of Christ. This was the consequence of the nobility of his nature and the holy union of human and divine nature in him. Therefore I say that there has never been, nor shall there ever be, a saint who has not felt both the pain of suffering and the delight of joy.

s.p: That sounds more real to my experience. Pure equanimity in all circumstances is surely beyond us?

m.e: I shall never reach the point where a hideous noise is as pleasing to my ears as sweetly sounding strings. But this much

is possible: that a rational God-shaped will may be free of all
natural pleasures and, upon hearing such a noise, commands
the sensual will not to be bothered by it, so that the latter
replies: 'I gladly agree!' Then conflict will turn to joy, for what
we must strive for with great effort becomes our heart's delight;
and only then does it bear fruit.

S.P: Can I ask about something else I hear? Because there are
those who say that they have advanced so far that they are free
even of good works.

M.E: This cannot be.

S.P: Because?

M.E: It was after receiving the Holy Spirit the disciples first
began to practice virtues.

S.P: And as you have said before, it's about the integration of
our inner and outer life; they flow in and out of each other.

Meister Eckhart's hooded head nods slowly and deliberately.

M.E: The external work, its size and extent, length and
breadth, cannot increase the quality of the inner work to any
degree whatsoever; since this is quality in itself. Thus the outer
work can never be minor, when the inner work is a major one;
and the outer work can never be good when the inner work
is without value. The inner work always determines in itself
all the dimensions of the outer work, its whole breadth and
extent. The inner work receives and draws the whole of its
being from nowhere but the heart, and in the heart of God.
There it receives the Son and is born as the Son in the womb
of the heavenly Father. But this is not the case with the outer
work, which receives its divine goodness through the inner
work; as something given and poured out via the descent of

the Godhead which then becomes something else – something dressed as distinction, number and divisibility, all of which properties are remote from God and alien to him.

s.p: I'm also aware that you've said, and I hope I'm quoting you accurately: 'What we take in, in contemplation, we pour out in love.'

m.e: Be sure of this, that if someone acts in such a way that their actions diminish other people, then they are not acting on the basis of God's kingdom. And this is also true: when works are performed purely from our human nature, they are troubled and agitated. When we act within God's kingdom, we are at peace in all that we do. But if our works are rooted in ourselves, then they are not perfect, for works in themselves are multiple and bring us into multiplicity, which is why we are often troubled in what we do.

I tell you truly: all that we do outside the kingdom of God is dead, but if we act within God's kingdom, then our works shall live. Therefore the prophet said that God no more loves his works than he is troubled and changed by them. And the same is true of the soul when she acts from the basis of God's kingdom. Whether such people act or refrain from acting, they remain the same, for their works are neither given them nor taken from them.

s.p: You compare our soul to God, and I want to return to that. But as our discussion of the spiritual life closes, perhaps some final words on prayer? I see, for instance, some novices being taught there in the East Cloister. What would you say to a novice on arrival at the monastery?

Meister Eckhart stands up and walks around a little, as if seeking wisdom. He speaks from the arched window, a dark silhouette against the bright sunlight outside.

M.E: There are nine things that we should bear in mind with respect to the words of prayer.

S.P: Nine?!

Meister Eckhart ignores my interruption.

M.E: Firstly, they have God as their object and receive their character from him. Secondly, they have been given us by God through Holy Scripture which was inspired by the Holy Spirit, and thus something divine has been stamped upon them. Thirdly, they express something of God and commend it to us, namely his mercy, his justice and so forth, his paternal nature and his love. Fourthly, the name of God is often uttered in prayer, which is sweet on the lips of those who love and is powerful for those in need. Fifthly, prayer is a conversation with God, and lovers take great delight in exchange that is intimate and secret. In the sixth place, the words of prayer often bring us to see our personal failings, as well as those of human nature, so that we are perhaps humbled in ourselves. In the seventh place, the vanity, fakery and inconstancy of the world are frequently considered and recalled, creating within us a disdain for the world. In the eighth place, the misery of the damned or of sinners is sometimes brought to mind. In the ninth place, the blessedness of the saints is often evoked, thus awakening our desire.

Truly, after that list, I feel like the novice, as I see for the first time the Dominican Master in action. I am suddenly compelled to ask one final question.

S.P: And are you happy?

Meister Eckhart looks up into the sky, and his eyes stay transfixed there as he speaks.

M.E: God is happy in himself; and all creatures, which God must make happy, will enjoy the same happiness as God, and in the same manner that he is happy. But be sure that in this unity, the spirit transcends every mode, even its own eternal being, and together with the Father soars up into the unity of the divine nature where God conceives himself in absolute simplicity. There, in that act, the spirit is no longer creature, but is the same as happiness itself, the nature and substance of the Godhead, the beautiful attitude of its own self and all creatures.

Some apple juice from the monastery press is brought to us, and we take a break. The bell will soon call us to Sext. In the meantime, however, Eckhart leaves me to consult with a figure who has been loitering awhile. It turns out to be Henricus de Cigno, the Dominican provincial of Teutonia, who will accompany him to Avignon tomorrow, along with three lectors. Certainly he has the support of those around him, which must be of some consolation; but you never know with Eckhart. As for myself, I check my notes; and then wander across to the vegetable garden, where a young monk works.

THREE

Soul

*I suspect that many working in this monastery garden do not
realize how daring Eckhart is with his theology. They find
him inspiring to listen to, without perhaps being aware of the
controversial ground that he treads – particularly in relation
to God and the soul. It is Eckhart's claim, for instance, that the
ground of God and the ground of the soul are one and the same;
and these are not words the church hierarchy wishes to hear.
By claiming that the human soul is continuous with divinity,
as opposed to separate from it, Eckhart puts himself outside the
Nicene Creed – the normative statement of belief for the Roman
Catholic Church since 381AD.*

*In brief, Eckhart stands accused of saying there is something in the
soul that is uncreated and uncreatable; and that it stands outside
time just as God stands outside time. The implication then is that
God did not create the soul, because the soul is part of God.*

*As always in mystical writing, there is strong emphasis here on the
absorption of the self into God in a unitive experience. But does
Eckhart go further and say that in fact, the two are one? Such is
the accusation.*

*I'm told you should never judge someone, until you have spoken
with them, person to person. And I have that chance now, as the
hazy afternoon heat holds sway in the cloisters where we sit. The
book work continues in the south cloister; and beyond the walls,
the fields of Cologne spread out far into the distance.*

s.p: I've been talking with Brother Paul in the vegetable
patch. He recounted a conversation he had with you, in which
he asked this question: why did the indescribable God, God
the all-highest, take on flesh?

M.E: I remember.

S.P: And what was your reply?

M.E: Why did the indescribable God take on flesh? In order that God may be born in the soul, and the soul be born in God.

S.P: And you believe this to be the reason for the incarnation of Christ on earth?

M.E: Indeed. That is why the whole of scripture was written and why God created the whole world and all the orders of angels: so that God could be born in the soul and the soul in God.

S.P: So the incarnation was about union; a union between God and the human soul?

M.E: The union of God with the soul is so great it is scarcely to be believed.

S.P: And this union – is it a future or present thing?

M.E: There is an inner work which neither time nor space can support or hold, and in which there is something divine and akin to God which is similarly beyond time and space. This inner work is equally present in all times and in all places, and is like God to this extent: no creature can wholly embrace it, and its goodness no creature can possess in itself. Therefore there must be something more inward and elevated, something uncreated, with neither boundaries nor mode of being, on which our heavenly Father can imprint himself, pouring himself forth, by which means he reveals himself: as Son and Holy Spirit.

s.p: You speak here of the soul as something uncreated and beyond time?

Meister Eckhart nods.

m.e: If someone possessed the skill and the power both to draw time and all that has happened in time during the past 6000 years or will happen before the end of time – and capture it in the now of the present, then that would be the 'fullness of time'. This is the now of eternity in which the soul knows all things new and fresh and present in God with the same delight which I have in those things that are present to me now.

s.p: So past, future and present are all as one for the soul – the eternal now?

m.e: There exists only the present instant; a now which always and without end is itself new. There is no yesterday, nor any tomorrow, but only now, as it was 1000 years ago and as it will be 1000 years hence.

s.p: So creation – which we sometimes think of as a one-off event, a long time ago – was not a one-off event at all, but is something continuous, endless and always?

m.e: I recently read in a book – who can fathom this? – that God is creating the world even now as he did on the first day when he created the world. So the soul which is to be born in God must fall away from time, as time must fall away from her. She must rise up and linger in contemplation of this wealth of God, where there is length without length, and breadth without breadth. There the soul knows all things and knows them in perfection.

s.p: God's wealth of being is expressed in an endless and

spilling heaven?

M.E: What the masters tell us about the dimensions of heaven defies belief, yet the least power in my soul is broader than the heavens, not to mention the intellect, in which there is a breadth without breadth. In the head of the soul, which is the intellect, I am as close to a point a thousand miles beyond the sea, as I am to the place where I presently sit. In this endless expanse and wealth of God, the soul attains knowing; no thing escapes her and she seeks nothing more.

S.P: You ask us to leave the shackles of time.

M.E: If I am to hear God speaking in me I must be wholly estranged from all that is mine; as strange as I am to things under the sea, and especially from time.

S.P: In other words, estranged from all created things?

M.E: The soul remains as young in her self, as when she was made. And I made a statement yesterday which seems almost incredible.

S.P: What was that?

M.E: I said that Jerusalem is as near my soul as the ground my feet touch now. Truly, a thousand miles beyond Jerusalem is every bit as nigh my soul as my own body is, of that I am as sure as of my being a man; and really, to any learned clerk it is not hard to understand. My soul is as young as when I was created; no, younger even! And I tell you, I should be ashamed were she not younger to-morrow than to-day!

S.P: Turning back the hands of time. And what powers does this ever-young soul have?

M.E: The soul has two powers which have nothing whatever to do with the body – namely the intellect and will, which both function above time. Oh, if only the soul's eyes were opened so that her understanding might behold the truth! Then it would be as easy for someone to give up everything as is it to give up peas and lentils! Yes, and upon my soul, to that person all else would be but vanity. There are some, you see, who give up things for love – yet still greatly prize what they leave.

S.P: They've given it up; but keep harking back to it.

M.E: But to the person who knows in truth, it matters not one whit that he should leave himself and everything; for anyone who takes this course already has all things for his own in truth.

S.P: I understand. But someone might imagine you were saying God is nowhere in the world, except in the soul. But isn't God in all things?

M.E: God is in all things as being, as activity, as power; but he is procreative in the soul alone. For although every creature is a glimmer of God, the soul is the natural image of God. No creature is susceptible to the birth of God, but the soul.

S.P: We don't perhaps realize how powerful and fertile our soul is?

M.E: The soul is scattered all over the place by her powers; and dissipated in the action of each. Thus her ability to work inwardly is enfeebled, for a scattered power is imperfect.

S.P: We allow our soul to be distracted?

M.E: The outer man is the swinging door; the inner man is the still hinge.

s.p: That's a good image. Because the swinging door is seen by everyone, while no one notices the hinge. Yet the hinge makes all things possible for the door, and without it there is nothing. At the heart of the hinge is stillness and simplicity –

Meister Eckhart swats away a fly, and coughs. The air is dry, and I pour him some more apple juice.

– and in like manner, our soul is gathered through simplicity and stillness. So tell me: is this something within everyone's power?

m.e: The spirit flows forth from all those who are children of God to a greater or lesser degree; from those who are transformed within God and bear his likeness in some manner. These people are removed from all multiplicity – which can still be found in even the highest angels; removed from all that allows even the merest hint or shadow of distinction, by being thought or named. These people are devoted to the One, who is free of all multiplicity and distinction, in which God-Father-Son-and-Holy-Spirit relinquishes, and is stripped of, all distinctions and properties and is one.

s.p: Let me be clear here. You are saying that behind the distinctions and labels of the Trinity, is in fact a oneness that knows no distinction and no labels; and our oneness with this oneness is our home?

Meister Eckhart is suddenly animated, speaking with some frustration.

m.e: This is my constant complaint! That unintelligent people who neither possess nor have any part of the Spirit of God wish to understand with their primitive reason what they read or hear in the Scripture, and so do not consider the words: 'What is impossible for men, is possible for God.' And this is no less true of the natural sphere: what is impossible for our lower nature is customary and natural for our higher nature.

s.p: But Margaret Porete – wasn't she burned at the stake in Paris for saying similar things? She also spoke of this fusion between God and the soul?

Meister Eckhart doesn't reply, keeping his thoughts private on this occasion. What was his awareness of this brave mystic? He had arrived in Paris in 1311, just a year after her execution. And he lived in the same Dominican convent as her inquisitor, William Humbert. I suspect their two paths never crossed; but he certainly will have known her famous work 'Mirror of simple souls', which became popular across Europe. I decide not to pursue the matter, however.

m.e: We should know first of all that we possess in ourselves two natures, one that is body and the other spirit. To the outer man, there belongs everything which, while it relates to the soul, is nevertheless enclosed by flesh, mixed up with it and which cooperates with each and every faculty of the body, such as the eye, the ear, the tongue, the hand and so forth. All this, Scripture calls the old, the earthly, the outer, the hostile or the slavish man.

s.p: And the other person in us?

m.e: The other person in us is the inner man, which Scripture calls the new, the heavenly, the young, the noble man or the friend. Even pagan masters, such as Cicero and Seneca, speak of the nobility of the inner man, who is the spirit, and the worthlessness of the outer man, who is the flesh. They say that no rational soul can exist without God and that the seed of God is in us.

I am struck by the duality of his words. For one so committed to the oneness of ultimate truth, he separates the two natures very cleanly. It appears as something of a contradiction, but he is already considering some words of St Augustine, a man he often quotes.

M.E: Augustine says that the first stage of the inner or new man is achieved when we live according to the example of good and holy people, even though we still clutch at chairs, lean against the walls and still drink at the breast.

The second stage comes when we no longer consider external images, even those of good men and women, but instead, run towards the teaching and wisdom of God, turning our back on the world and our face towards the divine. Then we clamber off our mother's lap and smile at our heavenly father.

The third stage is reached when we increasingly withdraw from our mother, removing ourselves from her lap. We shed concern and fear, so that even if it were in our power to inflict evil and injustice on all people without difficulty, we would not desire to do so, since through love, we are so gripped by God in eager devotion that he leads us in joy and sweetness and blessedness to where all that is unlike God and alien to him is hateful to us.

Eckhart is now counting each stage on the fingers of his raised hand.

The fourth stage arrives as we become ever more rooted in love and God, so that we are prepared to take upon ourselves any trial, temptation, discomfort and suffering willingly and gladly; eagerly and joyfully.

The fifth stage is when we live altogether at peace in ourselves, quietly resting in the overflowing wealth of the highest and unutterable wisdom.

s.p: And that's it?

m.e: The sixth stage –

s.p: – The sixth stage??

m.e: The sixth stage comes when we are stripped of our own form and transformed by God's eternity. Here we become wholly oblivious to all transient and temporal life, drawn into and changed into an image of the divine, and truly God's child. There is no stage higher than this, and here eternal peace and blessedness reign, for the end of the inner man and the new man is eternal life. The image of the divine nature and essence, God's Son, is revealed so that we become aware of him.

s.p: But the divine image is an image we can lose sense of?

m.e: Let me use a metaphor: the image of God, God's Son, is in the ground of the soul like a spring of living water. When someone throws earth upon it -that is earthly desire – then the spring becomes choked and blocked so that we no longer see it or know that it is there. And yet it still remains active and living in itself; and if we remove the earth with which it has been covered, then it appears again and we can see it.

s.p: I understand.

m.e: Or another picture: when a master sculpts a figure from wood, he does not place the figure in the wood – but carves away the sections that hide and conceal it. He gives the wood nothing, but rather takes from it, cutting away the excess, and then polishing what is discovered beneath. This is the treasure which lay hidden in the field, says our Lord in the gospel.

s.p: And what of grace? How is grace at work in the creation and growth of our inner selves? Can we expect help – or is it all hard work and striving?

M.E: The effect of grace is to make the soul buoyant and responsive to all the works of God, for grace bubbles up from the divine spring. It is a likeness of God, has a divine aroma, and makes the soul like God. Now when this grace and aroma enters the will, we call it love; and when this grace and aroma enters our intelligence, we call it the light of faith. And when this grace and aroma enters the irascible part of us – that is, the dynamic power of our gut – then we call it hope. That is why they are called divine virtues, since they have divine effects in the soul; just as we can tell by the power of the sun that it stirs the earth, awakening all things and sustaining their being. If this light were to disappear, then all else would disappear, and it would be as it was before they existed. And it is just the same with the soul: where there is grace and love, it is easy for us to do all godly works, and it is a sure sign of the absence of grace if we find it difficult to perform such things. It is nonsensical, for instance, for some people to fast and pray a good deal, to perform great works and seek constant solitude, if they remain restless and irritable, and do not improve their moral behaviour. They best take note of where they are weakest, and apply themselves to overcoming this. If their way of life is right, then God will be pleased with whatever they do.

S.P: You describe grace as a wonderful gift; a mysterious lubricant of the inner life, easing away friction and dissonance and liberating good works into the world.

M.E: Grace does not perform any works; it is too subtle for that, and is as far from performing works, as heaven is from earth. It is an indwelling; an inhering and a union with God; that is what grace is and there God is with you; and that is where birth occurs.

s.p: Can everyone experience this grace and this continual birth of God in their lives?

m.e: No one should think that it is impossible to get this far. There are some who say they do not have his grace. To these I reply: 'I'm sorry, but do you ask for it?' 'No.' 'Then I regret that even more.' Even if we cannot have grace, we can at least desire it. And if we cannot desire it, then we can at least have a desire to have a desire for it some day!

Meister Eckhart looks round; I feel he has had this conversation even here in the monastery. I gather my notes, and decide upon a fresh tack.

s.p: You sometimes speak of the soul's essence?

m.e: In created things, as I have often said before, there is no truth. But there is something which is above the created being of the soul and which is untouched by any createdness, and by any nothingness. Even the angels do not have this, whose clear being is pure and deep; for even that does not touch it. It is like the divine nature; in itself it is one and has nothing in common with anything else. And it is with regard to this that many teachers go wrong. It is a strange land, a wilderness, being more nameless than named; and more unknown than known. If you could do away with yourself for a moment, then you would possess all that this place possesses in itself. But as long as you have regard for yourself in any way, or for any thing, then you will not know what God is. As my mouth knows what colour is, and my eyes what taste is: this is how little you will know of what God is!

s.p: You are a keen follower of Plato, and I hear his influence in these words of yours.

m.e: Plato, the great priest, speaks to us of wonderful things.

He speaks of a purity that is not of the world. It is neither in the world, nor outside the world; neither in time nor in eternity, and has neither an exterior nor interior dimension. But from this purity, God the eternal Father, breathes forth the abundance and depths of his whole Godhead.

s.p: Which leads me onto the light in the soul, of which you often speak. Indeed, no offence, but people do say you're always mentioning it in your sermons!

m.e: Yes, I constantly return in my sermons to this light. A light both uncreated and uncreatable; and which apprehends God without medium, without any hiddenness and nakedly, just as he is in himself. I can again say truthfully that this light has more unity with God than it does with any of the soul's faculties, although it co-exists with these.

s.p: So is this light our noblest and best part?

m.e: No, this light is not nobler in the being of my soul than the lowest or most basic faculty, such as hearing or sight or some other of the senses which fall victim to hunger or thirst, cold or heat. This is because of the homogenous nature of being.

The homogenous nature of being? Meister Eckhart appears now to be turning his back on duality; and returning to the oneness of things.

s.p: You're encouraging us away from divisive labels again; asking instead that we consider ourselves as whole people; people who are one and undivided, and with no higher or lower parts?

m.e: In so far as we consider the soul's faculties in their being, they are all one and are equally noble. But if we consider

them according to their function, then one – the spark – is far
nobler and more elevated than another. Therefore, I say that
the extent to which we turn from ourselves and created things,
is the same extent to which we are united with the soul's spark,
which is untouched by either space or time.

s.p: And where does this spark take us?

m.e: This spark is opposed to all created things, desiring
nothing but God, naked, just as he is in himself. Neither is he
satisfied with the Father, Son or Holy Spirit, nor with the three
persons together, as far as each exists in their individuality. I
say truly that this light is not satisfied with the unity of the
divine nature. Indeed, I will say something that sounds even
more astonishing: I declare that by the good and eternal truth,
this light is not even satisfied with the simple, still and divine
being which neither gives nor takes! Rather, it desires to know
from where this being comes. It wants to penetrate to the
simple ground to the still desert, into which distinction never
entered – neither Father, Son nor Holy Spirit. There, in that
most inward place, where everyone is a stranger, the light is
satisfied at last; and there it is more inward than it is in itself,
for this ground is a simple stillness which is immoveable in
itself. However, all things are moved by this immovability and
all the forms of life are conceived by it.

There is no process, you see, of becoming in God; but only
a present moment. It is a becoming without becoming; a
becoming-new without renewal and this becoming is God's
being. There is in God something so subtle that no renewal
can enter there; and something so subtle in the soul, that is so
pure and fine, that no renewal can enter it either: for all that is
in God is an external present moment without renewal.

I ask if I might briefly stretch my legs. I wish to consider these
words, and so walk back to the vegetable garden. I pause

a while, contemplating the bare earth before me; and the simple ground of God, where label and distinction have never entered. Is that really my home? In a while, I return to the cloisters. Eckhart hasn't moved.

s.p: Can I now change tack a little, Meister and speak about anger? I noticed a while back you seemed quite angry. You were complaining about unintelligent people who didn't understand what was before their eyes. Do you remember?

He does, with a smile.

And of course we know that Jesus sometimes got angry and aggressive. In the temple, for instance, he evicted the traders, pushing over tables. Just why was he so angry on that occasion?

m.e: He wanted the temple to be empty. It was as if he had said: 'This temple is mine by right and I wish to have it to myself and to have command of it!'

s.p: How do you mean?

m.e: This temple, in which God wants to hold sway according to his will, is the human soul, which he formed in his own likeness. This is what he did. He made the human soul so similar to himself that neither in heaven nor on earth, among all the remarkable creatures which God created, is there one which is as like him as the human soul. This is why God wishes the temple to be empty; so that there is nothing there except him self. He feels so much at home in the temple; whenever he is alone in it.

s.p: I see.

m.e: So that is why the Lord drove the traders out of the

temple. The light and the darkness cannot exist together in the same place. God is truth and light in him self. So when God enters the temple, he banishes ignorance which is darkness, and reveals him self with light and truth. When the truth is known, the merchants vanish, of course, for truth does not desire any kind of trade-off. God does not seek his own interests but in all his works is unhampered and free and acts from pure love. And the same is true of that person who is united with God. They too are untethered and free in all their works, performing them for God alone, not seeking their own interests; and God works in them.

Thus when the temple becomes free of hindrances – that is, from attachment to self and ignorance – it is so sparklingly clear, and shines so beautifully both above all that God has made and through all that God has made, that no one can match its brilliance but the uncreated God alone. And in truth, the temple is like no one and nothing else but the uncreated God.

s.p: And staying with scriptural references, Meister, in a sermon about Mary the mother of Jesus, I heard you say that only a virgin can receive God, and I have to say, I was a little surprised. For what of those who are not virgins? Are we to be denied God?

m.e: 'Virgin' means someone who is free from all alien images; as free in fact as that person was before he or she existed.

s.p: Ahh! I see! But is that possible? How can someone who has lived a full life, and knows many things, be free of images? They will be full of them, surely?

m.e: Now take note of the following point: If I possessed such great intelligence that all the images anyone had ever conceived, together with all those which are in God himself, existed in my mind, but in such a way that I was free of any ego-attachment to them in what I did or in what I refrained from doing, but rather I remained free and empty in this present moment for the most precious will of God, constantly ready to fulfil it – then I would be a virgin unburdened by any images, just as certainly as I was before I existed.

s.p: So sexual experience does not deny us experience of the divine! I'm relieved to hear that, for we cannot all be monks with their vow of chastity. But tell me – this soul, even the soul free of image, does still seem to look in two different directions.

m.e: The soul has two eyes: an inner eye and an outer eye. The inner eye of the soul is the one which perceives being and receives its own being directly from God: this is the activity which is particular to itself. The outer eye of the soul is that which is directed towards all creatures and which perceives them in the manner of an image, by the use of a faculty. But they who are turned within themselves so they know God according to their own taste and in their own being – these people are freed from all created things and quite secure in themselves in a fortress of truth. Just as I once said that on Easter day, our Lord came to his disciples through locked doors, so too God does not enter those who are freed from all otherness and createdness; rather he already exists in an essential manner within them.

s.p: You are ambitious for the human soul.

m.e: When the soul receives a kiss from the Godhead, she stands in absolute perfection and blessedness, embraced by unity. By the touch of God, the soul is as noble as God himself.

s.p: So tell me – what prevents us from hearing these things? I mean inwardly hearing them.

m.e: There are three things that prevent us from hearing the eternal word. The first is the body; the second is multiplicity and the third is time. If only we could transcend these three, we could dwell in eternity, in the spirit, in the unity and in the desert, and there we would hear the eternal word.

I am conscious of some birds nesting in the cloister eves above our heads. They have been coming and going all day, but now a squawking squabble breaks out, full of fury and panic, and fluttering of wings. It is in contrast to Eckhart's calm demeanour; surprising for a man in his situation.

s.p: There is a great sense of equanimity in your words, Meister; an acceptance of circumstances, whatever they may be. And yours are not all they might be now.

Just for a moment, Meister Eckhart looks the old man who he is; weary if the fight, and given up to the will of others.

So people will want to know: how is such equanimity acquired?

m.e: There is in the soul a power that finds all things equally pleasing. In fact, the very worst and very best things are exactly the same for this power, which receives everything from above, which is the here and now.

So receive what God wishes to give you in the moment, remaining always in humility and absence of self, and always remembering that you are quite unworthy of any good which God might give you; if that should be his wish. The fact that good is hidden from us is entirely our own fault. We are the cause of all our problems, so guard yourself against yourself, and you will be safe. And even if we do not wish to accept his love, he has nevertheless chosen us for this. If we do not accept it therefore, we shall regret it and shall be sorely punished. As I say, the fact that we do not arrive at the place where this good is received is not his fault but ours.

The birds are quieter now; the conflict appears to have been settled.

S.P: Some quick questions, Meister, as time ticks on, even in the eternal now: what would you say to someone who feels alone in the spiritual life; perhaps an island even?

M.E: In spiritual things, one thing is always in another. That which receives is the same as that which is received, for it receives nothing other than itself. This is difficult. Whoever understands it has been preached to enough.

S.P: So another question: how is the soul formed? Some people say it's born of will or knowledge; that these things determine its image?

M.E: No. The image of the soul is the product of itself, with neither will nor knowledge. Here's an analogy. When a branch grows from a tree, it bears the name and nature of the tree. What grows out is the same as what remains within, and what remains within is the same as what grows out. Thus the branch is an expression of itself.

S.P: How does the soul make it to God; or receive God?

M.E: The soul has three ways to God. The first way is to seek God in all created things, with countless actions of burning love. The second is the pathless way, which is free and yet fixed, in which we are raised and exalted above ourselves and all things, with neither will nor images; although not yet a substantial being. Christ was referring to this when he said: 'You are blessed, Peter. Flesh and blood have not enlightened you, but being caught up in the higher mind. When you call me God, my heavenly Father has revealed it to you.' But even Peter did not see God as he truly is; although he was raised up to the circle of eternity beyond all created understanding by the power of his heavenly Father.

S.P: And the third way?

M.E: Although the third way is called a 'way', it is also reminiscent of 'being at home'. It is seeing God directly in his own being. This transcends anything that can be said in words. Listen to this miracle! How astonishing to be within and without, to grasp and be grasped, to see and be ourselves seen, to hold and to be ourselves held – that is the goal, where the spirit dwells in peace, united with precious eternity.

S.P: So can good works ever help us draw near to God?

M.E: Three things are essential to the works we perform; and these are that we should act in an orderly way, and with insight and perspicacity. By orderly, I mean that which corresponds to the highest in all its aspects; and by insight, I mean that which for the time being is the extent of our understanding. And finally by perspicacity, I mean sensing in good works the joyful presence of the living truth. Where all three of these things coincide, they draw us as close to God and are as life giving as all the raptures of Mary Magdalene in the desert.

S.P: Yet Christ famously says 'only one thing is necessary'. What is this one thing?

M.E: It is God. This is what all creatures need, for if God took back what belongs to him, all creatures would fall into nothingness. If God removed what is his from the soul of

Christ, where his spirit is united with the eternal person, then Christ too would be no more than a creature. Therefore we have a great need of the one thing.

s.p: You have spoken often this afternoon of God uniting with the soul. Can you describe this simply?

m.e: The closest parallel we can find is that of body and soul. They are so united with each other that the body cannot act without the soul, or the soul without the body. God is to the soul as the soul is to the body and when the soul departs from the body, the body must die. So too must the soul die if God departs from her.

s.p: So can the soul help itself in this union?

m.e: There are three obstacles which hinder the union of the soul with God. The first is that she is too scattered and is not unified in herself, since the soul is never unified when she inclines to created things. The second is that she is mixed with transient affairs. The third is that when she is turned to the body, she cannot be united with God. On the other hand, there are three things which further the union of God with the soul. The first is that the soul is unified and undivided – simple, as God is simple in himself. The second is that she is raised above herself and all transient things, holding rather to God. The third is that she is separated from all material things and acts from her primal and original purity.

s.p: And in some way, you say this amazing soul must die?

m.e: To die, properly understood, is nothing other than the ending of all that is. I do not mean that the being of the soul falls into nothingness as she was before she was created; rather we should understand this ending to be the removal of possessing and having. Here the soul forsakes all things, both

God and creatures. Of course, it sounds astonishing to say the soul should forsake God, but I assert that it is more important for the soul to forsake God to attain perfection, than it is for the soul to forsake creatures. The soul must exist in a free nothingness. And fear not: that we should forsake God is altogether what God intends, for as long as the soul has God, knows God and is aware of God, she is far from God.

s.p: Really?

m.e: This then is God's desire – that God should reduce himself to nothing in the soul, so that the soul may lose her self. For the fact that God is called God comes from creatures. When the soul was a creature, she had a God, and then as she lost her createdness, God remained for himself as he is. And this is the greatest honour that the soul can pay to God, to take leave of God; to be free of him.

s.p: So let me understand: while the soul is still giving God names, she is in some way separating herself from God; and not completely one with God?

m.e: The soul must die to all the divine activity which we attribute to the divine nature, if she is to enter the divine essence where God is free of all his work. For the highest image in the soul sees the essence of the Godhead without means; the place where it is free and empty of all forms of work. Therefore this highest image should guide the soul; but it should also die with her.

s.p: Because all images must pass; even the best ones.

m.e: When the soul has left her created being; and then from the uncreated being in which she finds herself, has entered the divine essence where she cannot comprehend the kingdom of God – then the soul discovers herself, goes her own way and never seeks God; and thus she dies her highest death. In this death, the soul loses all her desires, all images, all understanding and form, and is stripped of all her being.

S.P: It sounds both terrible and wonderful.

M.E: And be sure of this, by the living God: just as a dead person, a corpse, cannot move themselves, neither can a soul who has experienced this spiritual death, present an image or a particular way of being towards anyone else, since this spirit is dead and now buried in the Godhead.

Meister Eckhart is suddenly on his feet again, and passionate.

O noble soul, consider your nobility! For until you have entirely abandoned your self, and cast your self into the bottomless ocean of the Godhead – you cannot know this divine death. Remember! The soul must remain in death and must not flinch from death!

And with that he strode away towards the chapel. In a while, the bell would call the community to None, the mid-afternoon office. I decided not to join them, choosing instead to wander in contemplation round the back of the infirmary. I had much to reflect on, and needed silence rather than the recitation of psalms. There's a season for everything.

FOUR

God

All mystics face the same problem when trying to communicate
their experience; for the origins of the mystic experience lie both
beyond conscious thought and beyond the bounds of human
language. How then to speak of it? In the attempt to say the un-
sayable, most mystics turn to symbols. They create symbols around
which their ideas can gather. The symbol itself is not the ultimate
truth; for truth cannot be named. But the symbol speaks some of
the truth, enshrining an aspect of the mystery; and is as specific as
language can be.

Hugh of Saint Victor (1096–1141) was one such mystic; and
with his writings widely available across the libraries of Europe,
Eckhart will have been well aware of him. Hugh understood
the dilemma facing mystics: 'It is impossible to represent
invisible things except by means of those which are visible,' he
said. 'Therefore all theology of necessity has recourse to visible
representations in order to make known the invisible.'

Eckhart shared Hugh's understanding of symbols. He knew of
their importance; but knew also of the need to get beyond them. It
was in his reflections on God that this tension is most evident. He
wishes to say clear and understandable things about things that
are not clear and understandable; and this leads him into perhaps
his most provocative language and thought, particularly as he
considers the Trinity. So I am looking forward to this particular
session. First, however, as we settle on our seats, I address an issue
which has just arisen in the monastery kitchens...

s.p: I've just been speaking with Brother Gabriel in the
monastery kitchen. We were talking about his life here, and
the various responsibilities he has; tasks which he must fit in
around the eight daily offices. All very interesting; and then he

told me about his name. He says he took that name from the angel Gabriel who visited the Virgin Mary to announce what was to be. And it made me wonder, by way of nothing at all: do all the angels have names?

Meister Eckhart proves rather dismissive of my suggestion.

M.E: The angel's name was no more Gabriel than it was Conrad.

S.P: It might be kind not to tell him that; he's quite proud of it.

M.E: No one can know the angel's name. No master and no mind has ever penetrated to the place where the angel is known by name, and perhaps indeed it has no name. The soul too is nameless, by the way. It is no more possible to find a name for the soul than it is to find one for God, even though some weighty tomes have been written about this! But in so far as she chooses to act, we give her a name. Consider a carpenter for instance. This is not so much his name as the name of what he does and of which he is master. 'Gabriel' took his name from the act which he proclaimed, since 'Gabriel' means 'power'.

S.P: Well, with that little kitchen query cleared up, how are we to approach God in our discussion? It is hard if, as you say, God is to remain nameless.

M.E: God in himself is so far above that no form of knowledge or desire can ever reach him. Desire is deep, immeasurably so. But nothing that the intellect can grasp, and nothing that desire can desire, is God. Where understanding and desire end, there is darkness and there God's radiance begins.

s.p: Yet you have just returned from None, and in a while will attend Vespers! Is this not you seeking God both in form and through rituals?

m.e: To seek God by rituals is to get the ritual and lose God in the process, for he hides behind it. On the other hand, to seek God without clever device is to take him as he is, and so doing, a person lives by the Son and is the life itself.

I may have looked quizzical at this point; he seemed to feel the need to explain.

You should understand that all external works which we may practice serve only to constrain nature; they don't remove it. In order to eradicate nature it is spiritual works that we must perform. Now there are many people who rather than denying themselves, actually maintain themselves in their own self-esteem. But truly, all these are deceived, for this is contrary to so many things – contrary to human reason, contrary to the experience of grace and contrary to the testimony of the Holy Spirit! I will not say that those who hold external observance to be the best shall be damned; but only that they shall not come to God without great purification in purgatory. For these people do not follow God, if they do not abandon themselves; rather, they follow the self-esteem in which they hold themselves.

s.p: You do not appear to be a great fan of external observances.

m.e: God is no more likely to be found in external observances than he is in sin.

s.p: I'm sure the Pope will appreciate that observation.

m.e: Yet these people, those who delight in external

devotions, have great status in the eyes of the world, which comes from their likeness to it. For those who understand only physical things, have a high regard for the kind of life which they can perceive with the senses. Thus one ass is adored by another.

I'm warming to this man. But soon I am being taken back to the soul's essence.

We should understand the function of the inner self, which is contemplation in knowledge and love. It is here that the beginning of a holy life lies. And with these activities of knowledge and love the essence of the soul is described. If we can only comprehend this essence in these two powers, then these are the noblest activities which exist in us.

S.P: So God isn't mediated through other things?

M.E: Every kind of mediation is alien to God. God says 'I am the first and the last'. There is neither distinction in God nor in the persons of the Trinity according to the unity of their nature. The divine nature is one, and each Person is both one and the same One as God's nature. The difference between essence and existence is apprehended as one. Difference is born, exists and possessed only where this oneness no longer obtains. Therefore it is in oneness that God is found, and they who would find God must themselves become one. In labels which separate, we find neither oneness, essence, God, rest, blessedness or contentment. Be one then, so that you shall find God! And truly, if you are properly one, then you shall remain one in the midst of difference, and the many and separate will be one for you and shall not be able to impede you in anyway. The one remains equally one in a thousand times a thousand stones, as it does in four stones; and a thousand times a thousand is just as certainly a simple number as four is a number.

S.P: So if we are inwardly one; any amount of multiplicity we may experience in life is also lived as one. We should perhaps become simpler people?

M.E: To be full of things is to be empty of God. To be empty of things is to be full of God. You have to start first with yourself, and leave yourself.

I was aware that one of Eckhart's favourite Jesus sayings, was this: 'He who would save his soul, must lose it.'

God must act and pour himself into us when we are ready, in other words, when we are totally empty of self and creatures. So stand still and do not waver from your emptiness.

S.P: We are invited to be people who exist only in God, seek oneness only with God, and take this stripped-down attitude into the multiplicity and variety of life?

M.E: A pagan master says that the one is born from the all-highest God; it is his nature to be with the one. Whoever seeks oneness at a point beneath God, deceives themselves.

S.P: So our attempts at oneness with created things, those things at a point beneath God, are at best misguided, and at worst, destructive of our spiritual health?

M.E: The masters say that the power through which the eye sees is quite different from that through which it knows it sees. The former, the seeing, is something which it takes from the colour, rather from that which is coloured. Thus it is of no consequence whether that which is coloured is a stone or a piece of wood, a person or an angel: the essential thing is only that it has colour. In the same way I say the noble person derives their whole essence, life and happiness solely from God, with God and in God – and not from knowing, seeing or loving God or anything of that kind; not in knowing that they know God. For how should we know ourselves to know God, when we do not even know ourselves?

s.p: Good point.

m.e: Indeed, it is not ourselves and other things that we know, but rather God alone, if we rest in the root and ground of blessedness. But when the soul knows that she knows God, then she has knowledge simultaneously of God and of itself.

s.p: Everyone has to start somewhere, though; with things they can understand and know. You do tend to demand the impossible.

m.e: It is true that here below, in this life, that power by which we know and understand that we see, is nobler and better than that power by which we see, since nature begins her work at the weakest point while God begins his at the point of perfection. Nature makes a man and a woman from a child, and a chicken from an egg, while God makes the man or woman before the child and the chicken before the egg. Nature first makes the wood warm and then hot, and only then does she generate fire, while God first gives all creatures being and only later, within time and yet timelessly and individually, he gives them all that belongs to being.

s.p: So we were being, before we were creature – and that is still how God perceives us. The trouble is, though, as creatures, those familiar with this world, it's much easier for us to relate to nature which is all around us, than to God, as nature works in time and in a realm of knowing, which we can understand.

m.e: Of course. But although there cannot be happiness without conscious awareness that we see and know God, God forbid that our happiness should be founded on this. If someone else is happy with this, then all well and good, but I do not want it. The heat of fire and the essence of fire are quite different from each other, and are astonishingly far apart by nature, even though they exist in close proximity within time and space. Seeing God and seeing ourselves are wholly separate and distinct. One with one, one from one, one in one and one in one in all eternity. Amen!

He is holding up one finger, and repeatedly hitting the air with it, laughing. But its time for me to raise another matter; one which I'm sure the Pope will also have views on.

S.P: I'm aware that your talk of the Trinity has caused some controversy. Many are disconcerted by it, because it is not traditional Christian teaching.

M.E: If there were a hundred persons in the Godhead, they would see only one God. Unbelievers and some uneducated Christians are astounded at this; even some priests know as little about it as a stone does, and take three in the sense of three cows or three stones. But whoever can conceive of distinction in God without number or quantity, knows that three persons are a single God.

S.P: And so talk of the Trinity is unhelpful?

M.E: In the oneness of God, the divinity of God is perfected. I say this: that God could never give birth to his sole-begotten Son if he were not one. All that God works in creatures and in his divinity, God derives from his oneness. I say further that God alone possesses oneness. That is the defining characteristic of his being, and it is on account of this that God is God. Everything which is multiple depends on the one, but the one depends upon nothing. The wealth and wisdom and truth of God are entirely one in God; and not just one, but also oneness. But we are different – we want one thing and then another! Now we practice wisdom and now some art or other. It is because the soul does not possess the one, that she will never find rest until all things are one in God. God is one; this is the happiness of the soul, her adornment and her peace.

S.P: And the angels? They may not have names – but can they help?

M.E: They proclaim God's kingdom just as a king is proclaimed by his number of knights. For this reason he is known as the Lord of hosts. But however exalted they may be, this whole host of angels must assist and cooperate with God, if God is to be born in the soul. This means they have delight, joy and bliss in the birth, though they do not bring it about. No creature can bring it about, since it is the work of God alone and the angels can only serve him in it.

S.P: So how is God, God? God is one – but what defines this nameless presence?

M.E: Do you know how God is God? God is God because there is nothing of the creature in him. He has never been named within time.

S.P: Whereas much of the creature is caught up in time?

M.E: Creatures, sin and death belong to time, and in a certain sense they are all related. But since the soul has fallen away from time – if indeed she has fallen away from the world – then there is neither pain nor suffering there. Indeed, even tribulation turns to joy for her there. If we were to compare everything which has ever been conceived of, regarding delight and joy, bliss and pleasure, with the delight which belongs to this birth, then it would all be as nothing.

S.P: So wait a minute: getting back to God – if God is

nameless and uncreated, where is God?

M.E: God is in all things.

S.P: But how so? How is the uncreated God in created things?

M.E: The more he is in things, the more he is outside them: the more in, the more out and the more out, the more in! I have already said on a number of occasions that God created the whole world perfectly and entirely in the now. And God still creates now everything he made six thousand years ago or more, when he created the world. God is in all things, but in so far as God is divine and in so far as God is rational, he exists more properly in the soul and in angels; that is, in the innermost and highest parts of the soul, than he does anywhere else. In that place, to which neither time nor the light of any image ever penetrated, in the highest and inner most parts of the soul, God creates the whole of this world. Everything which God created six thousand years ago and everything which he shall create over the next thousand years, if the world lasts that long, he creates in the innermost and highest part of the soul. Everything which is past, present and future, God creates in the innermost part of the soul.

S.P: And is this a God who we can pray to?

M.E: As I was sitting somewhere yesterday, I repeated a phrase taken from Our Father: 'May your will be done'. But it would have been better to say, 'May will itself be yours' – that my will may be his will and that I may be him. This is what the prayer means.

S.P: A merging of wills; not easy. Any advice?

M.E: Be asleep with respect to all things! In other words, know nothing of time, creatures or images. The masters say: if someone who is soundly asleep were to slumber for a hundred years, then they would have no knowledge of any creature, of time or images. And then you could become aware of what God is doing within you.

s.p: So what should we call the nameless God? Surely we have to call God something in order to enter into a relationship? Or do we just refer to him as the God with no name?

m.e: God has many names in scripture. But I say that if someone perceives something in God and gives it a name, then that is not God. God is above names and nature. We read of a good man who turned to God in his prayer and wished to give him a name. Then a brother said: 'Be silent! You are dishonouring God!' There is no name we can devise for God. But some names are allowed – names which the saints have used and which God has made sacred in their hearts and bathed in a golden light.

s.p: So the call is something like: 'Name God; but sit light to the name'. Which makes me wonder how we are to approach God?

m.e: We should say, 'Lord, with the same names which you have so consecrated in the hearts of your saints and bathed in your light, we approach you and praise you.' Secondly, we should learn that there is no name we can give God which praises him or honours him adequately, since God is above names and beyond words.

s.p: You almost seem to be saying: the less said about God the better?

m.e: Now pay attention to this –

Eckhart leans forward.

— God is nameless, for no one can either speak of him or know him. Accordingly, if I say 'God is good', this is not true. I am good, but God is not good! In fact, I would rather say that I am better than God, for what is good can become better and what can become better can become the best! Now God is not good, so he cannot become better. Since he cannot become better, he cannot become the best. These three are far from God, 'good', 'better' 'best', for he is wholly transcendent. If I say again that God is wise, then this is not true. Or if I say that God exists, this is also not true. He is being beyond being: he is a nothingness beyond being. Therefore St Augustine says: 'The finest thing we can say of God is to be silent concerning him from the wisdom of inner riches.' Be silent therefore, and do not chatter about God, for by chattering about him, you tell lies and commit a sin. If you wish to be perfect and without sin, then do not prattle about God.

s.p: I do try not to prattle. Anything else we should avoid?

m.e: Also you should not wish to understand anything about God, for God is beyond all understanding. If you understand anything about him, then God is not in it; and by understanding something of him, you fall into ignorance; and by falling into ignorance, you become like an animal, since the animal part in creatures is that which is unknowing. If you do not wish to become like an animal therefore, do not pretend that you understand anything of the indescribable God.

s.p: What then should I do?

m.e: You should sink your being into his being. Your you and his him should become a single me, so that with him you shall know in eternity his unbecome being and his unnameable nothingness.

s.p: It is hard to love nothingness. So how should I love God?

M.E: You should love God without your head; that is to say, the soul should become headless and stripped of her mental nature. For as long as your soul is mental, she will possess images. As long as she has images, she will possess intermediaries, and as long as she has intermediaries, she will not have unity or simplicity. As long as she lacks simplicity, she does not truly love God, for true love depends on simplicity. Therefore you soul should lose all mental nature and be left headless, for if you love God as 'God' or as 'spirit' or as 'person' or as 'image' – well, all this must be abandoned. You must love him as he is a non-God, a non-spirit, a non-person, a non-image. Indeed, you must love him as he is one, pure, simple and transparent, and far from all duality. And we should eternally sink into this one, thus passing from something into nothing.

S.P: Heaven sounds quite expensive, in a way.

M.E: On the contrary, heaven is cheap because it is on sale to everyone at the price they can afford.

Encouragement stirs in my battered psyche. But I have an ethical concern to raise now.

S.P: Meister Eckhart – how do you know what God's will is? If God is indescribable, then surely his will is indescribable?

M.E: My answer is that if it were not God's will even for a moment, then it would not exist.

I gesture at all around me, both near and far.

S.P: So everything around us – the sun, the weeds, the cracked flag stones – this is all God's will?

M.E: Whatever is, must be his will. If God's will is pleasing to you, then whatever happens to you, or does not happen to you, will be quite perfect. Those who desire something other than God's will get their just desserts, for they are always in trouble and misery. They must constantly endure violence and injustice, and suffering is their perpetual lot. And this is rightly so, since they act as if they were betraying God for money, as Judas did. They love God for the sake of something else; something which is not God. And when they get what they want, they have no further concern with God.

s.p: So if God's will is whatever is, is there nothing fresh to expect from God? It seems hard that we should desire neither blessing nor consolation.

m.e: Be certain of this: God never ceases to give us everything. Even if he had sworn not to, he could still not help giving us things. Indeed, it is far more important for him to give than it is for us to receive. But we best not focus on this, for the less we strive for it, the more God will give us. God intends by this only that we should become richer still and be all the more capable of receiving things from him. Sometimes, for instance, it is my custom when I pray, to say these words: 'Lord, what we ask you for is so small. If someone asked me for it, then I would do it for them, and yet it is a hundred times easier for you to do than for me, and your desire to do it is greater too. And if we were to ask you for something greater, it would still be easy for you to give it. The greater the gift, the more willingly you give it.' God is ready to give us great things if only we can renounce everything.

s.p: Only when we're a blank canvass can his likeness become imprinted on our soul?

m.e: I have often said the following which is a sure truth: if someone was famished to the point of death and was then offered the finest food, if God's likeness was not in it, then they would prefer to die rather than taste or enjoy it. And similarly, if this person were freezing to death, they could not touch or put on any type of clothing – unless God's likeness was in it!

s.p: Now that's what I call purity of heart!

m.e: Indeed. Purity of heart is being detached and removed from all physical things, gathered and enclosed in oneself, and then springing forth from purity into God and being united there.

s.p: Moving on, you suggest that creation should delight in God. But does God delight in us?

m.e: If we take a fly as it exists in God, then it is nobler in God than the highest angel is in itself. Now all things are equal and alike in God, and are God. And this likeness is so delightful to God that his whole nature and being floods through himself, in this likeness. This is as delightful for him as when you let a horse run free in a green field which is completely flat and even. It is the horse's nature to expend its energy in springing and bucking in the meadow: this is his delight and accords with his nature. In the same way it is delightful for God to find likeness. It is a pleasure for him to pour out his nature and his being into likeness, since likeness is what he himself is.

s.p: I'm enjoying the idea of God as a delighted horse running freeing a flat green field.

m.e: And now I will say something I have never said before.

s.p: A moment while I sharpen my quill.

m.e: God delights in himself. In the delight in which God

delights in himself, he delights also in all creatures. Not as creatures; but in creatures as God. In the delight in which God delights in him self, in that same delight he delights in all things.

s.p: So the attraction is one way?

m.e: While God is not drawn to creatures, since he sees only himself, creatures are indeed drawn to God, since all that has ever emerged from God looks back to him.

I am aware our time is nearly done; and the afternoon sun on the wane, lengthening the cloistered shadows. But there is one more feature of Eckhart's thought I need to speak about.

s.p: Meister, I'm aware of an important distinction you make, when you talk about God; and its one that might surprise many.

Eckhart innocently raises his eyebrows.

You distinguish between God and the Godhead. What is the difference between them?

m.e: All that is in the Godhead is one, and of this no one can speak. God acts, while the Godhead does not act. There is nothing for it to do, for there is no action in it. It has never sought to do anything. The difference between God and the Godhead is that one acts, and the other does not.

s.p: So hang fire just for a moment while I think out loud: you're saying that because of our entrapment in our time-bound and multiple selves, God is revealed to us a person who acts. But – and it's a big but – behind this revelation, this appearance, is the unrevealed Godhead, the 'ground' of God, who is above and beyond all description and distinction; the one you call 'The Nameless Nothing'.

Eckhart nods.

Can the enlightened soul see this Godhead?

M.E: Whenever the soul sees anything that is imaged, this is an imperfection in her. Even if she sees God, in so far as he is 'God', or in so far as he is something imaged or triune, this also is an imperfection in her. But when all images are removed from the soul and she perceives the single oneness, the pure being of the soul, resting in her self, then she receives the pure formless being of divine unity which is being beyond being. O miracle of miracles!

Both Eckhart's arms are held up in the air; his palms skywards.

What a wonderful receptivity it is when the being of the soul can endure nothing but the pure unity of God.

S.P: So it's seeing without seeing. And as we retreat from the world of image, to a place of utter sparseness, so we experience the birth of God in our soul.

I look at my notes, and see one more question. In a way, he has answered it already. But who knows, something else might emerge?

And so finally, Meister Eckhart, have you anything more to say to the question: what is God?

M.E: In the fifth book of On Contemplation Bernard writes: 'What is God?' And answers: 'That being in comparison with which nothing better can be conceived.' And Seneca asks: 'What is God?' And answers: 'All that you see and all that you cannot see. Thus the greatness attributed to him is such that nothing greater can be conceived.'

s.p: So that's Bernard and Seneca. But what do you say?

m.e: God is infinite in his simplicity and simple in his infinity. Therefore he is everywhere and is everywhere complete. He is everywhere on account of his infinity, and is everywhere complete on account of his simplicity. Only God flows into all things, penetrating their essence. Nothing else flows into something else. God is in the innermost part of each and every thing; in fact, only in its innermost part, and he alone is one. And someone who truly loves God as the one, and for the sake of the one and of oneness, is not at all concerned with his power or wisdom, for these things are multiple and relate to multiplicity. They are not even concerned with his goodness in general. Oneness is higher, prior and simpler than goodness itself.

s.p: Meister Eckhart, thank you. We will meet for the final time after Vespers.

FIVE

Suffering

We have eaten with the community in the refectory. Meat is forbidden in the kitchens, but we enjoyed fish, and the weak beer I have become familiar with in monasteries. We ate in silence, which I found surprisingly pleasant.

I had attended Vespers, and been struck afresh by our final psalm – Psalm 22. It was this psalm which Jesus quoted on the cross: 'My God, my God – why have you forsaken me?' The verse goes on: 'Why are you so far from helping me and from the words of my groaning?' It focused my mind on the conversation to come.

I have not spoken directly with Eckhart about his feelings at present; it has not felt appropriate. My assumption is that if he wishes to speak of them, he will. So does he feel betrayed by Mother Church? Abandoned by her? Or just misunderstood? Is his current predicament as nothing to him? Or does it weigh heavily? I don't know; but I do know that I bring the questions of many as we sit down now for our final session together.

There is a slight chill in the air, as evening beckons; a candle burns on the table – a harbinger of the darkness to come.

s.p: In our final conversation, Meister, could you start by describing the nature of our suffering? We tend to lump all suffering altogether, but I suspect it isn't so.

m.e: There are three kinds of suffering which affect and oppress us in this place of exile. The first comes from damage to our worldly goods; the second from any harm which befalls our relatives and friends, and the third comes from the injury we suffer when we become the objects of others' disdain; or when we experience hardship, physical pain and emotional distress.

s.p: That seems a pretty good summary. So is there a way of being which will take us away from pain?

m.e: A wise man and wisdom; and true man and truth; a just man and justice; a good man and goodness relate to one another in the following way. Goodness is neither created nor made, but is simply produced in a good man. Thus a good man, in so far as he is good, is himself unmade and uncreated; while goodness reproduces itself and all that it is in him.

s.p: Like attracts like.

m.e: Indeed. Goodness pours knowledge, love and activity into a good man and the good man receives the whole of his being, knowledge, love and activity from the heart and core of goodness and from it alone. So a good man and goodness are nothing but a single goodness, wholly one in all things, except for the producing on the one side, and the receiving on the other. A good man receives everything which belongs to him from the goodness in goodness; and makes it his home. It is there that he knows himself and knows everything that he knows, and loves every thing he loves.

s.p: Forgive me, but what has this to do with suffering?

m.e: Everything which I have just said concerning a good man and goodness is no less true of a true man and truth, a just man and justice, a wise man and wisdom, God the Son and God the father – indeed of all who are born of God and have no father on earth; those in whom nothing created is born and in whom there is no image, but only God, naked and pure. Thus I say that in God there is neither sadness, nor suffering, nor distress, and if you wish to be free of all distress and suffering, then turn to God and fix yourself on him alone. If you were formed and born solely in justice, then truly nothing could cause you pain, any more than justice can cause God pain.

S.P: I think I see. Our suffering comes from a place that has not been formed by God; a place that somehow stands outside his in-filling? That suffering in God is in fact impossible.

Meister Eckhart nods, and is quick to step in.

M.E: Thus we should strive to shed our form and the forms of all creatures, knowing no father but God alone. Then nothing shall be able to cause us pain or oppress us, neither God nor any creature, neither things created nor uncreated, and our whole being, life, awareness, knowledge and love will be from God and in God and indeed will actually *be* God.

S.P: I'm aware that we're susceptible to different sorts of pain. What particularly hurts one person, may not so threaten another. So does the nature of our pain tell us something about ourselves? And of course some people are impossible to console, full stop.

M.E: If the loss of external things causes me pain, then this is a clear sign that I love external things and thus, in truth, love suffering and despair. I turn to created things which, by their nature, are the source of suffering, whilst turning my back on God, from whom all consolation comes. Is it then surprising that I suffer and that I am sad? Truly, it is impossible for God and for the whole world to console someone who seeks consolation from that which is created. But they who love only God in the creature, and the creature only in God —well, they will find true and constant consolation in all places.

No one can be good who does not will exactly what God wills; for it is impossible that God could will anything other than the good. Seneca, a pagan master, asks: 'What is the best consolation in suffering and distress?' and gives this answer: 'It is this: that we should accept everything as if we had desired it and prayed for it, for you would have desired it, if you had known that all things happen from, with and in the will of God.'

s.p: That's a positive approach to suffering; but also one that some of us will struggle with. It demands blind trust in the darkness; when we might be looking for a hand held out in help.

m.e: No hardship or loss is without some gain, and there is no harm which is wholly negative. God always creates and gives some consolation for – as the saints and pagan masters also tell us – neither God nor nature allows such a thing as unadulterated evil or suffering. Let us suppose that someone had one hundred marks, forty of which they lose and sixty of which remain in their possession. Now if they think constantly of the forty which they have lost, then this person will remain restless and depressed. Indeed, how could they be comforted and forget their suffering, while they cling to their bad fortune and their suffering – brooding on it, gazing upon it, as it gazes back at them; talking and conversing with it as the loss does with them, each staring the other in the eyes. But if, on the other hand, they were to consider the 60 marks which they still have, turning their back on the 40 which were lost, immersing themselves into the 60, staring *them* in the eyes and talking to them – hah! Well, then they would certainly be comforted! What exists and is good can offer us comfort; while what does not exist and is not good – that which remains as 'mine' and 'of me' – must necessarily cause heart ache, suffering and disappointment. So when suffering and distress come knocking at your door, consider the good and pleasing things which you still possess.

s.p: I suppose self-pity is inclined to look round at others, noting all the things they appear to have.

m.e: If you want to be comforted, then forget those who are better off than you and think always of those whose fate is worse.

s.p: And in some manner, forget also those things which we love – if that does not sound too strange?

m.e: It is another kind of consolation: if someone has lost an external possession of theirs, whatever it may be – a friend or relative, an eye, or a hand – they should know that if they patiently suffer this loss for God's sake, they will at least possess before God all that for which they would not have wished to lose it. If for instance someone loses their sight in one eye, and if they would not have wished to lose the sight of this eye for a thousand marks or six thousand marks or even more, then they will certainly possess with God all that they would have given in order not to endure such suffering or loss.

s.p: Suffering helps us give value to things.

m.e: And this is what our Lord must have meant when he said: 'It is better for you to enter into eternal life with one eye, than be lost with two.' Or, 'He who leaves father and mother, sister and brother, farm and fields or anything else, shall receive back a hundredfold and eternal life.' Certainly I dare to say by God's truth and by my salvation that whoever leaves their father and mother, brother or sister for the sake of God and goodness, will receive back a hundredfold in two ways. The first is that their father, mother, brother and sister will become a hundred times dearer to them than they are now; and the second is that not only a hundred people, but in fact everyone will become incomparably more precious to them than either their father, mother or brother are precious to them at present. The fact that someone is not aware of this can only mean that they have not yet left their father, mother, sister or brother for God's sake, still possessing them on earth in their heart; that is, if they are those who still become depressed and troubled about what is not of God, and attentive to it.

S.P: So we let go; and receive back something greater.

M.E: You should know, however, that people possess different degrees of both virtue and the will to suffer; just as we see in nature that one person is bigger, or more attractive in form, complexion, knowledge or skills than another. And I say this too that someone can be good, and yet still be swayed to a greater or lesser degree by their natural love for their father, mother, sister or brother. They are good and better to the extent that to a greater or lesser degree, they are consoled and affected by it, and are conscious of their natural love and affection for father and mother, sister and brother and for themselves.

S.P: We need to be aware of our different allegiances in the world and how they affect us. After all, wasn't it Jesus himself who asked: 'Who is my mother?' But amidst it all, we are always within reach of God in this present moment, through trust?

M.E: Of course. If, for instance, a thief is able to endure his death entirely, truly, perfectly, willingly and happily out of love for God's justice – in which and according to which, God wills that the criminal should be put to death – then he would certainly be saved and would be blessed.

The light is fading. The hour of Compline approaches; the night prayer. Brother Gabriel kindly replaces our candle with a fresh one, the tallow recently cut. I enjoy the aroma of fresh wax, as Gabriel disappears into the shadows. Meister Eckhart continues to speak – though in a way, as one talking to himself.

We should also consider in our suffering that God speaks
the truth and that his promises are founded upon himself as
truth. And his word is that our sorrow shall be turned into joy.
Now truly, if I knew that all the stones in my possession were
going to turn into gold, then the more stones I had, and the
bigger they were, the happier I would be! Indeed, I would ask
for more stones and, if able, would get big ones and many of
them.

s.p: So our suffering should not lead us to regret the path
we've taken?

m.e: If someone were to take a particular path, set about
a particular task or even abandon one, and then were to
suffer an injury of some kind – perhaps they might break
a leg or an arm, or lose the sight of an eye, or fall ill – then
if they constantly think to themselves 'If only I had taken
another path, or set about another task, this would never have
happened to me!' – then they shall remain without consolation
and will necessarily be grief-stricken. Therefore they should
think to themselves: 'If I had taken another path or if I had
set about or had abandoned another task, then I might easily
have suffered even greater misfortune.' And thus they will be
comforted.

s.p: Hindsight is not always a friend.

m.e: And another point which can bring us consolation. If
it were the case that someone who had possessed honour and
comfort for many years now lost those things by divine decree,
then this person best reflect wisely and thank God.

s.p: Thank God?

M.E: When they become aware of their present injury and
hardship, they will realize for the first time how wonderful was
their earlier advantage and security. And so they best thank
God for this security previously enjoyed; for at the time, they
had not been aware of how fortunate they were; and so they
should stop complaining. And since all that is good, consoling
or existent in time is only on loan to us, what right do we have
to complain if the one who lent it to us, wishes now to take it
back again? No, we should thank God he has lent it to us for
such a long time. And we should thank God for not taking
back all that he has lent us; for it would be perfectly just
for God to take back all that he has lent us; especially if we
become indignant when he takes from us just a part of what
has never been ours, and of which we have never been the true
owner.

S.P: A spirit of gratitude is a beautiful virtue. And particularly
found in those who have a sense of God creating presently;
creating now, just as much as at the beginning of time.

M.E: God loves for his own sake and performs all things for
his own sake, which means to say that he loves for the sake
of love and he acts through his works for the sake of acting;
for without doubt, if God had never given birth to his only
begotten Son in eternity, then having given birth in the past
would not be the same as giving birth in the present. Thus
the saints say that the Son is born eternally and that he will
continue to be born without ceasing. And neither would God
have created the world, if *having* created were not the same as
still creating. Therefore God created the world in such a way
that he still creates it without ceasing. All that belongs to the
past and future is remote and alien to God.

There is noise again from the nest above us; but these are more
peaceful sounds.

This is why I have said that the good person desires to suffer for love, not to *have suffered* for love: it is suffering in the present that brings them what they love. Thus they are God's son or daughter, formed in God and in his own image, who loves for his own sake, which means to say that he loves for the sake of love and acts for the sake of acting, and so God loves and acts without ceasing. God's acting is his very nature, his being, his all, his happiness.

s.p: So our suffering is to be considered a present act of creation; something in which God is actively present now, creating something now, and leading us somewhere now?

m.e: Our Lord says: 'Anyone who wishes to be a follower of mine must renounce self; take up his cross and follow me.' But this is not only a commandment, as is usually said, but is also a promise and a divine instruction, as to how the whole of our suffering, action and life can be turned to bliss and joy, and it is more a reward than a commandment. For such a person has everything they desire, since they desire nothing which is bad, and this is happiness.

s.p: Some people say that suffering is a divine punishment.

m.e: I know. And now we can see the stupidity of those who are much struck by the fact that good people suffer pain and hardship; and who then conceive the idea this is the result of their hidden sins. Sometimes they even say: 'Oh, I thought so-and-so was a good person! How is it they now suffer so much pain and hardship? And I thought they had no vices!' But if they are good, their suffering is neither pain nor misfortune, but is rather great good fortune, and their happiness.

s.p: And can we speak of God sharing our suffering?

m.e: I say the fact that God is with us when we suffer means

that he himself shares our suffering. Indeed, whoever knows
what truth is, knows that what I say now is true. God shares
our suffering; indeed, he suffers in his own way more readily
and more deeply than they who suffer for his sake.

s.p: Yet the cynic will say: so what? So what if he shares our
suffering? How does that help?

m.e: A friend's compassion naturally lessens our suffering. If I
am consoled when another person shares in my suffering, then
I will be comforted even more if it is God who suffers with me.

s.p: So given all you have said about the benefits of suffering,
I'm now wondering this: should we ever ask to be healed? It
is, after all, a very natural request. But you leave me a little
confused.

m.e: One reason why it would be both pointless and
belittling for me to ask God to make me well again, is that
I am reluctant to ask such a rich, loving and generous God
for something so insignificant as this. Supposing I travelled
to see the Pope one or two hundred miles away, and said as I
stepped before him, 'Holy Father, I have made a difficult and
costly journey of two hundred miles to beseech you to give
me a single bean!' He himself and anyone standing nearby
would justifiably say I was a complete fool. But it is a certain
truth that everything good – even the whole of creation – is
less beside God, than a single bean is beside the whole of the
physical world. That is why I rightfully hold back from asking
God to make me better; if I am good and wise.

s.p: Your pain is too insignificant to mention, and your
request, ridiculously small?

m.e: A good and godly person should be heartily ashamed
of ever having succumbed to pain, when we consider that in

the hope of only a small reward and trusting to his luck, a merchant will journey miles abroad, traversing difficult paths, mountains and dale, desert and sea. His life and goods are constantly threatened by robbers and murderers; he suffers lack of food, drink and sleep, and other discomforts – yet does all this willingly for the sake of such small and uncertain profit. A knight in battle risks his possessions, his life and his soul for the sake of a glory that is brief and passing; and yet enduring just a little suffering for God and for eternal happiness seems such a big thing to us!

s.p: You say challenging things. Many will find your words both difficult to believe, and hard to put into practice. Who do you imagine will be most drawn to your words?

m.e: Whoever has abandoned the whole of their will, will appreciate my teaching and understand my words.

s.p: And finally, Meister, now our time is done – give us please a simple word to live by.

Eckhart is taken unawares, and pauses for a moment.

m.e: What does it avail me if the birth is always happening, if it does not happen to me? That it should happen to me is what matters!

s.p: Thank you for your time. Shortly, the bell will call us to Compline, and I know you have a long journey to make in the morning.

I gather up my notes, as he rises from his seat.

If nothing else, Meister, you have reminded me that I don't pray enough.

He looks down at me, his hooded face a-flicker in the candle light.

M.E: If the only prayer you say in your life is 'thank you', that would suffice.

And with that, he disappears into the cloister shadows. I do not see him again. I decide against Compline, retiring early to my lodgings. I have some images to dismantle.

SIX
Afterword

The day after we spoke, Meister Eckhart set off for the Papal Court in Avignon. He made there a brave defence of his faith, claiming the charges against him were lodged out of jealousy and pursued out of ignorance. He died the following year, however, 1328, before the process was complete. Some believe that January 28th was the day of his death: the feast of St Thomas.

Even in death, the Archbishop of Cologne pursued his vendetta against Eckhart. Using his political leverage over the Pope, the Archbishop insisted on an official condemnation. A 'papal bull' was duly issued, describing Eckhart as 'evil-sounding, rash and suspect of heresy'; while also censuring him for having misled 'the uneducated crowd' by his teaching and preaching. He was not formally declared a heretic, but was accused of sowing 'thorns and obstacles contrary to the very clear truth of faith in the field of the church' and 'working to produce harmful thistles and poisonous thorn bushes.'

Eckhart's reputation was seriously wounded by this papal pronouncement; his memory was tainted, and his teachings suppressed. Many of his writings were lost or destroyed, and remarkably for a man of his stature, his burial site has never been discovered. Even his own Dominican Order dropped a veil of silence over the episode; and aware of establishment hostility, attempted to rein in their more adventurous teachers. Truly, Eckhart had been abandoned by the church he had sought to serve.

But not everyone gave up on Eckhart. Henry Suso and John Tauler were perhaps his most famous students, incorporating his thought into their teaching; and with Jan van Ruus Broec, these four became known as 'The Rhineland Mystics'. They were one in their search for that which was most essential in religion; for its profoundest and most inward dimensions: the indwelling of God in the soul; and the indwelling of the soul in God.

Meanwhile, the nuns of South Rhineland committed many of his sermons first to memory, and then to written record; whilst the friars in Cologne copied out nearly 600 excerpts from his commentary of St John's Gospel. His teaching was also kept alive by a circle of spiritual friends who became known as *The Friends of God*. Eckhart's body was dead, but his thoughts were alive; renounced by the powers; but cherished by his followers.

Eckhart's teaching is an adventure, not a system; a call, not a creed. The depth and universality of his work means it can be contained by no established religion, but draws to itself seekers of truth from all backgrounds. Here we have a teaching open to all, but possessed by none; and therefore free like a butterfly, in the garden of the soul.

Free.

And on reflection, that's my abiding memory of the man I met, all those years ago. He was free.

Simon Parke

Simon Parke was a priest in the Church of England for twenty years, before leaving for fresh adventures. He worked for three years in a supermarket, stacking shelves and working on the till. He was also chair of the shop union. He has since left to go free lance, and now writes, leads retreats and offers consultancy.

He has written for *The Independent* and *The Evening Standard*, and is currently columnist with the *Daily Mail*. His weekly supermarket diary, 'Shelf Life', ran for 15 months in the *Mail on Saturday*, and he now contributes another weekly column called 'One-Minute Mystic.' The book version of *Shelf Life* has recently been published by Rider. The book version of *One-Minute Mystic* is published by Hay House in January 2010.

Other books by Simon include *Forsaking the Family* – a refreshingly real look at family life. Our families made us; yet we understand very little of how our experiences as children still affects us. The book starts by contemplating Jesus' ambivalence towards his own family, particularly his parents; reflects on how our family settings can both help and harm us; and suggests paths for freedom and authenticity.

The Beautiful Life – ten new commandments because life could be better was published by Bloomsbury, and describes ten skilful attitudes for life. Simon leads retreats around this book, and talks about it on this site. It is now also available in audio form with White Crow books.

Simon has been a teacher of the Enneagram for twenty years. The enneagram is an ancient and remarkable path of self-understanding, and Simon's book on the subject, published by Lion, is called *Enneagram – a private session with the world's greatest psychologist*.

Another bloody retreat is Simon's desert novel, describing events at the monastery of St James-the-Less set in the sands of Middle Egypt. It follows the fortunes of Abbot Peter and the rest of the community, when the stillness of their sacred setting is rudely and irrevocably shattered.

Simon was born in Sussex, but has lived and worked in London for twenty-five years. He has written comedy and satire for TV and radio, picking up a Sony radio award. He has two grown-up children and his hobbies include football, history and running. For more information, visit his website www.simonparke.com

Also available from White Crow Books

Marcus Aurelius—*The Meditations*
ISBN 978-1-907355-20-2

Elsa Barker—*Letters from
a Living Dead Man*
ISBN 978-1-907355-83-7

Elsa Barker—*War Letters
from the Living Dead Man*
ISBN 978-1-907355-85-1

Elsa Barker—*Last Letters
from the Living Dead Man*
ISBN 978-1-907355-87-5

Richard Maurice Bucke—
Cosmic Consciousness
ISBN 978-1-907355-10-3

G. K. Chesterton—*The
Everlasting Man*
ISBN 978-1-907355-03-5

G. K. Chesterton—*Heretics*
ISBN 978-1-907355-02-8

G. K. Chesterton—*Orthodoxy*
ISBN 978-1-907355-01-1

Arthur Conan Doyle—*The
Edge of the Unknown*
ISBN 978-1-907355-14-1

Arthur Conan Doyle—
The New Revelation
ISBN 978-1-907355-12-7

Arthur Conan Doyle—
The Vital Message
ISBN 978-1-907355-13-4

Arthur Conan Doyle with
Simon Parke—*Conversations
with Arthur Conan Doyle*
ISBN 978-1-907355-80-6

Leon Denis with Arthur Conan
Doyle—*The Mystery of Joan of Arc*
ISBN 978-1-907355-17-2

The Earl of Dunraven—*Experiences
in Spiritualism with D. D. Home*
ISBN 978-1-907355-93-6

Meister Eckhart with Simon
Parke—*Conversations
with Meister Eckhart*
ISBN 978-1-907355-18-9

Kahlil Gibran—*The Forerunner*
ISBN 978-1-907355-06-6

Kahlil Gibran—*The Madman*
ISBN 978-1-907355-05-9

Kahlil Gibran—*The Prophet*
ISBN 978-1-907355-04-2

Kahlil Gibran—*Sand and Foam*
ISBN 978-1-907355-07-3

Kahlil Gibran—*Jesus the Son of Man*
ISBN 978-1-907355-08-0

Kahlil Gibran—*Spiritual World*
ISBN 978-1-907355-09-7

Hermann Hesse—*Siddhartha*
ISBN 978-1-907355-31-8

D. D. Home—*Incidents
in my Life Part 1*
ISBN 978-1-907355-15-8

Mme. Dunglas Home; edited,
with an Introduction, by Sir
Arthur Conan Doyle—*D. D.
Home: His Life and Mission*
ISBN 978-1-907355-16-5

Andrew Lang—*The Book
of Dreams and Ghosts*
ISBN 978-1-907355-97-4

Edward C. Randall—
Frontiers of the Afterlife
ISBN 978-1-907355-30-1

Lucius Annaeus Seneca—*On Benefits*
ISBN 978-1-907355-19-6

Rebecca Ruter Springer—*Intra
Muros—My Dream of Heaven*
ISBN 978-1-907355-11-0

W. T. Stead—*After Death* or *Letters
from Julia: A Personal Narrative*
ISBN 978-1-907355-89-9

Leo Tolstoy, edited by Simon
Parke—*Tolstoy's Forbidden Words*
ISBN 978-1-907355-00-4

Leo Tolstoy—*A Confession*
ISBN 978-1-907355-24-0

Leo Tolstoy—*The Gospel in Brief*
ISBN 978-1-907355-22-6

Leo Tolstoy—*The Kingdom
of God is Within You*
ISBN 978-1-907355-27-1

Leo Tolstoy—*My Religion:
What I Believe*
ISBN 978-1-907355-23-3

Leo Tolstoy—*On Life*
ISBN 978-1-907355-91-2

Leo Tolstoy—*Twenty-three Tales*
ISBN 978-1-907355-29-5

Leo Tolstoy—*What is Religion
and other writings*
ISBN 978-1-907355-28-8

Leo Tolstoy—*Work While
Ye Have the Light*
ISBN 978-1-907355-26-4

Leo Tolstoy with Simon Parke—
Conversations with Tolstoy
ISBN 978-1-907355-25-7

Howard Williams with an
Introduction by Leo Tolstoy—
*The Ethics of Diet: An Anthology
of Vegetarian Thought*
ISBN 978-1-907355-21-9

**All titles available as eBooks, and select titles available in Audiobook
format from www.whitecrowbooks.com**

Lightning Source UK Ltd.
Milton Keynes UK
24 March 2010

151820UK00001B/13/P